D0733612

Creative Postproduction

Editing, Sound, Visual Effects, and Music for Film and Video

Robert Benedetti, P.G.A.

Michael Brown, A.C.E.

Bernie Laramie

Patrick Williams

PEARSON

Boston ■ New York ■ San Francisco
Mexico City ■ Montreal ■ Toronto ■ London ■ Madrid ■ Munich ■ Paris
Hong Kong ■ Singapore ■ Tokyo ■ Cape Town ■ Sydney

LIST OF ILLUSTRATIONS

ABOUT THE AUTHORS

The four authors of this book are working professionals in the world of film and television. They have written out of their own broad personal experience in both feature films and television movies and programs. They speak not only of the techniques and processes of their work, but also of its esthetics, politics, and customs. They hope that as you share their insights and experiences, you will come to feel what it is like to do this work, work that often goes unnoticed and unrecognized except at private gatherings of peer groups or in the glare of the Emmys or Oscars, awards that are soon forgotten by everyone except the recipients and those who employ them.

Here are the authors, in the order in which you will meet them in this book.

ROBERT BENEDETTI, P.G.A., (General Editor) is a multiple Emmy and Peabody Award-winning producer of movies such as HBO's *Miss Evers' Boys* and *A Lesson Before Dying* and in 1997 was named Producer of the Year by the Producers Guild of America. He is the author of several books, including *The Actor at Work, The Actor in You, ACTION!: Acting for Film and Television,* and *From Concept to Screen: An Overview of Film and Television Production.* He taught acting, directing, and producing for many years at Carnegie-Mellon University, as Chairman of the Acting Program at the Yale Drama School, as Chairman of the Theatre Program at York University, and as Dean of Theatre at the California Institute of the Arts.

BERNIE LARAMIE (Postproduction and Effects) has been a producer specializing in postproduction for more than twenty-five years. He is best known for his work in such special effects series as *Max Headroom, Dark Skies, The Invaders, War of the Worlds,* and *CSI: Crime Scene Investigation.* After many years as an editor in sitcoms, corporate films, and commercials, Bernie became Director of Postproduction at Lorimar Studios in the mid-1980s, leading the transition from film to electronic postproduction there. He pioneered the use of many state-of-the-art techniques that are used today, including electronic nonlinear editing systems and computer graphics for special effects. Bernie was a consultant to Lucasfilm's Droidworks in the creation of the Editdroid editing system. He teaches Postproduction for Film and Television at UCLA Extension and has been a guest lecturer at USC, Cal Arts, and Santa Monica College. He is a member of the Editors Guild, the Directors Guild, and the Society of Motion Picture and Television Engineers (SMPTE).

MICHAEL BROWN, A.C.E. (Editing) is an Emmy Award-winning film editor. He has edited eight feature films, ten miniseries, thirty-seven movies for television, and several television series. He won an Emmy for Best Editing for HBO's *Miss Evers' Boys.* In addition, he edited two other movies that won the Best Picture Emmy and earned Emmy and A.C.E. nominations for several additional movies. He is a member of the

Writers Guild of America and the Directors Guild of America and has been a guest teacher at several Los Angeles schools.

PATRICK WILLIAMS (Music) is one of the most versatile composers in the music industry. Having composed well over 150 scores for theatrical features and television films, as well as records and concert works, Williams has received twenty-two Emmy nominations and twelve Grammy nominations and has been nominated for both the Academy Award (for *Breaking Away*) and the Pulitzer Prize. He went on to win four Emmys, two Grammys, and the prestigious Richard Kirk Lifetime Achievement Award from BMI. He has been actively involved in the field of music education, holding posts as Visiting Professor and Composer-in-Residence at the University of Utah and the University of Colorado, and has performed and lectured at the Berklee College of Music, Duke University, Indiana University, Texas Christian University (1993 Greens Honors Professor), UCLA, USC, and Yale University. He was awarded honorary doctorates by both the University of Colorado and Duke University. He is currently the Artistic Director of the Henry Mancini Institute at UCLA.

Acknowledgments

We would like to thank the reviewers of this edition for their thoughtful comments: Dennis Aig, Montana State University; John A. Duvall, Elon University; Cynthia L. Hill, University of Florida; Mary Jackson Pitts, Arkansas State University; and David Schmoeller, University of Nevada, Las Vegas.

INTRODUCTION

The Changing Role of Postproduction

ROBERT BENEDETTI

There is a saying in the movie industry, often attributed to Francis Ford Coppola, that a movie is made three times: once when it is written, again when it is shot, and a third time in postproduction. This book is about that "third making." It has been written to enhance understanding and appreciation of cinema in all its forms by anyone who loves it; to explain the creative aspects of postproduction to those who are headed for careers as directors, cinematographers, producers, or writers; and to inspire those who might want to pursue a career in the area of postproduction itself.

Many books have treated the technical and logistical aspects of postproduction. This book, however, is not a technical how-to manual, although many technical considerations are necessarily discussed along the way, in the same way that a book on painting would need to discuss pigment and brushwork.[1] The real aim of this book is to explore the creative aspects of the third making, the ways in which postproduction can be seen not only as a manipulation and enhancement of the material created during principal photography, but also as a continuation of the primary creative filmmaking process. According to *American Cinematographer* magazine, "'Postproduction,' which was once defined as shepherding a film through the lab and to the big screen, is today a highly elastic term that continues to be redefined by emerging markets and technologies."[2] Directors and cinematographers nowadays often work far beyond the completion of principal photography to manipulate the **look** of the film and to supervise the creation and incorporation of digital imagery, which makes up an increasingly significant part of many productions. Our aim, then, is to help you realize that nowadays, creativity continues to the very end of the filmmaking process. Understanding this will enrich and enliven your experience of watching films and television.

Note: Special terms will appear in **boldface** when they are first used. These and other terms are defined in the Glossary at the end of this book. Also, all films that are mentioned can be found in the Index of Films Cited, with dates and directors.

The Production Process in Brief

The production process is traditionally divided into three periods: Prep (preproduction), Shoot (also called principal photography), and Post (postproduction). In

---

[1]For the technical aspects of postproduction, we recommend Barbara Clark and Susan J. Spohr's *Guide to Postproduction for TV and Film,* Focal Press, 1998.

[2]Debra Kaufman and Ray Zone, "Legacy of Invention," *American Cinematographer,* May 2002, p. 64.

network TV and cable TV shows and studio films, however, a crucial preliminary phase—called Development—usually precedes production. This is the period during which a project is conceived, the script is written, and the money needed to produce it is found. This seemingly endless process (often called "development hell") usually involves acquiring options on the source material (e.g., books or life stories), hiring a writer, and having a script written and rewritten through several drafts (and perhaps several writers). Once the script has been approved, preliminary budgets are prepared. If the budget appears feasible, the project is scheduled for production. This is called getting the green light, though there still may be intermediate hurdles to be cleared, such as getting the commitment of an acceptable star or director; this is the dreaded condition known as the "flashing green light."

Even though rights and scripts can cost hundreds of thousands of dollars, surprisingly few developed scripts are actually made. In television, perhaps one in five projects that are developed is ultimately produced; in feature films, the ratio may be more like one in twenty. Even in the world of independent films, countless projects fall by the wayside before financing is arranged and the camera rolls.

Assuming that a project survives development, production itself finally begins with Prep, the period when a production office is opened, actors and crews are hired, locations are selected, designs are approved and sets are built, equipment is ordered, and everything else needed to shoot is put in place. Prep can be as short as three or four weeks for a television movie or can last many months for a feature film.

The Shoot is that whirlwind period of fourteen-hour days during which everything involving live actors is filmed, however much it may be augmented and altered later. Far more money is spent per day during the Shoot than at any other time, so the number of shooting days, called the *schedule,* is kept as short as possible: ten or twelve days for a low-budget independent film, eighteen to twenty days for a two-hour television movie, twenty-six to thirty days for a high-quality cable film, and sixty or more days for a feature (Sydney Pollack's *Out of Africa* shot for 100 days.)

Post is usually the longest of the three periods of actual production, lasting anywhere from a couple of days to two weeks for a sitcom, four to sixteen weeks for a television or cable movie, many months for a theatrical feature, and a year or more for a big **"effects"** movie. Post includes everything that may happen after principal photography has ended in order to complete and deliver the product and involves three main aspects of a show: the visual aspects, the auditory aspects, and the finishing of the final product.

In Post, the visual aspects of a show are completed first through the **editing** process. Although editing primarily involves arranging and manipulating the material that was filmed during the Shoot, nowadays it also involves the incorporation of special visual effects created simultaneously with and after the Shoot, such as computer-generated imagery (**CGI**) and composite effects created through various superimposition techniques such as **mattes** and **green screen.**

In fact, with the advancement of digital technology, it is becoming easier and easier to alter, enhance, and augment the visual material created during principal photography. As a result, the line between Shoot and Post has become indistinct. In a sense, the Shoot may now extend far into what was traditionally called the postproduction period. Increasingly, we not only finish and even "fix it in Post," we actually *create* it in Post.

Once the visual aspect of the film is fixed (when the **cut** has been **locked**), work begins on the auditory elements of the show. Although much has been done during editing to begin preparing these sound elements, they can be shaped for marriage with the picture only after the cut has been locked. The auditory aspects of a film include music and sound design. Music includes both the **underscore** (the music that is composed or selected to accompany and enhance the **action** and emotion of the picture) and the selection of **source music** (music from sources such as radios, jukeboxes, and phonographs). Sound design is concerned with all the nonmusical sounds of the film. These include the "hard" sound effects that are created to complete and enhance the action, such as gunshots, explosions, engine sounds, and thunder, as well as the creation of exotic sounds, such as the voices of the dinosaurs in the *Jurassic Park* movies. Sound design also includes improvements and adjustments to the dialogue by Automatic Dialogue Replacement (**ADR**) as well as environmental sound such as traffic, animals, and night sounds; human background sounds such as crowds and PA announcements (generically called **Walla**); and sounds related to the activity of the actors such as footsteps, door slams, kisses, and table noises (generically called **Foley**).

After all the sound and music have been married to the picture at the **final mix** (also called the **dub**), the final phase of work begins to render the show ready for **delivery.** This phase includes many technical processes such as **negative cutting** (unless the product has originated in video) and **transfers** of various sorts. If a film delivery is required, the show must be printed from the cut negative; for a video delivery, a digital master is created. In either case, the quality of the image is adjusted and enhanced through **timing** (nowadays often done digitally even when the final product is delivered on film stock). Finally, the optical or digital sound track is married to the final product.

Although this final phase of work after the dub is considered the most technical and least creative, the care and skill employed here can have a major effect on the finished product, especially in the matter of timing. All these postproduction processes are complex and require special skills and equipment. The coordination of this work, which goes on simultaneously in many separate places, is itself the specialized skill of the **postproduction supervisor.**

Post culminates in the **final delivery,** in which the show is handed over to the network, studio, or distributor in the exact form or forms required, along with (for film) the original negatives and the internegative and exhibition **print** or (for video) the source materials and video master. Final delivery also includes elements such as outtakes, cue sheets, releases, music scores, accounting records, and a mountain of other paperwork. The final payment of a large portion of the production budget and producers' fees is withheld until every item of the complex and legally required final delivery is complete.

This book covers the main creative aspects of postproduction. Part One gives an overview of the entire postproduction process with emphasis on new techniques. Part Two covers the esthetics and politics of editing. Part Three describes the composition of the music, a topic that is too often ignored in film classes and relegated to the music department; even though few of us will ever write music for a film, insight into this process will enhance the ability of any student of film to appreciate the power of film music and to work with a film composer.

Several topics overlap among the three parts of the book; several aspects of sound, for example, are a concern for the postproduction supervisor, the **editor,** and the composer. Though these topics are mentioned in each of the three parts, they are discussed most fully in the part associated with the person who most closely supervises the activity: Sound design and Foley are described in Part One as concerns of the postproduction supervisor and sound supervisor; ADR and Walla are covered in Part Two as concerns of the editor; scoring is covered in Part Three as a concern of the composer. The same principle applies to several other topics; digital and computer technology, for instance, is discussed in all three parts, each time from the point of view of that particular part.

Film versus Video

The low cost of digital production has brought filmmaking within everyone's reach. Many digital video cameras (DV Cams) are capable of producing **broadcast-quality** material, and video has become the medium of choice for almost all home and student work. Moreover, the infrastructure supporting digital production is improving all the time; some home computers, for instance, now come with serviceable digital editing programs installed, and even the popular **Avid** editing system is now available for home computers at a reasonable price.

In the professional arena, digital processes already dominate the world of postproduction because of their speed of execution and their infinite capacity for manipulation. The digital revolution is beginning to spread into the Shoot as well. As the versatility of digital cameras continues to improve, with increased resolution and exposure latitudes, interchangeable lenses, accurate monitoring systems, and variable **frame rates,** film stock will eventually become obsolete for most commercial purposes. Already, many television programs and even some made-for-television movies are shot, edited, and broadcast entirely in digital video. More and more theatrical feature films are being shot for High-Definition Television (**HDTV**) and then transferred to film stock for distribution. As digital projection systems become more common in theaters, film stock may someday be obsolete even for theatrical distribution.

Despite this move toward digital media and away from film, this book addresses both film and digital processes. This is for two reasons. First, any student of cinema should be aware of the historical development of the film medium, because many processes and terms that are still in use are inextricably bound to the development of film itself. Second, although the digital revolution is well underway, it is far from complete. The large majority of feature films and high-quality network and cable movies are still shot and delivered on film. Even most low-budget independent features are still being shot on film because of the high cost of transferring digital material to film stock for exhibition and distribution. Moreover, we predict that film stock will never entirely disappear for projects of the highest quality and for archival purposes. For all these reasons, a student filmmaker entering the market of the next decade will be severely limited by training that ignores film techniques.

Although digital video represents the most important technological advance since the invention of cinema, it doesn't change things much creatively. The fact that almost anyone can buy or rent a good digital camera, shoot something, and then sit at home and edit it doesn't mean that we will suddenly be glutted with talented filmmakers, any more than the wide availability of the automobile produced a society of Grand Prix racecar drivers. There are intangibles required, such as the storytelling instinct, visual talent, a sense of character, and the ability to coalesce the various elements that make cinema—the most inclusive of all the arts—into a unified whole. The best filmmakers will continue to be special people.

PART ONE

The Postproduction Process

BERNIE LARAMIE

Don't worry, we can fix it in post.
            —Countless Directors and Producers

1   Getting Started

More is changing today in motion picture production than at any time in the past thirty years. We are moving rapidly toward the end of the film era as it has existed for almost a hundred years and are just beginning the changeover to the world of digital technology.

Dailies from the Harry Potter movies, shot in England, were beamed via satellite to executives in Hollywood. In my own television work, digital dailies are shipped straight to my office from the set, arriving on the same day they were shot. Editors at Warner Brothers Studios in California are collaborating in real time with producers and directors of *The Third Watch* at the show's location in New York, using an interactive system provided by Pipeline Pictures. Films being **mixed** at LucasFilm in northern California are being reviewed in southern California via Private Data Networks. Patrick Williams is conducting recording sessions from Hollywood with a string section in Utah and singer Gloria Estefan in Miami, all linked by fiber-optic cable. In the near future, motion pictures will no longer be distributed on film, and most won't even be shot on film.

In the face of all this change, the postproduction supervisor's job is to bring these evolving technologies together within an environment that is conducive to human creativity. As the Volkswagen commercial says, "It's not rocket science. . . . Well, just a little."

Post Begins in Prep

Of all of the misconceptions about postproduction, the most common is that it begins "after the shooting stops."

The classic definitions of the three main phases of the filmmaking process as preproduction (or simply Prep), production (or simply Shoot), and postproduction (or simply Post) is traditional but unfortunately doesn't really work out quite so neatly in actual practice, and recent advances in technology have blurred the distinctions even more. In truth, Post actually begins in Prep, long before the Shoot starts, before the actors are cast, even before the locations are selected or the sets designed. This early planning for Post is essential.

When I was working on *CSI: Crime Scene Investigation,* our Technical Consultant, Detective Elizabeth Devine, always said, "People get caught not because they don't plan the crime well, they get caught because they don't plan what happens *after* the crime well." The same is true of filmmaking: Lack of planning for Post can damage all the cost and effort of Prep and the Shoot itself.

Here's an experience of mine that demonstrates this point. Some years ago, I was working with digital effects for television. We'd had digital capabilities in TV for years, and after my years in TV, I was eager to try my hand at some feature-quality work. I mentioned this to a friend. "Great," he said, "why don't you help me finish the effects on this feature we're doing?" "Sure," I said quickly—fantasy fulfilled. I went straight to his office to close the deal. The project consisted mainly of some effects to be created using a process called green screen, in which actors are filmed in front of—you guessed it—a green **background.** The picture is then run through a program that replaces the green background with another image (more on this later). I was excited. This was a process that we often used in TV, and I was confident I could produce good results at these higher levels of resolution. It would be basically the same, just more.

I have a couple of personal rules that I try to follow about the jobs I take. First, I never take on a project without meeting the director, however briefly. Second, I never, never take on a project without reading the script at least once. But this project was being offered by a friend who was one of the best effects producers in Hollywood, and besides, I was dying to try out the new Quantel Domino Effects Box I would be using. So I put aside my rules and signed on. It'll be fine, I told myself.

The next day was the last day of principal photography, and I visited the set to meet the director for the first time. We began talking about the effects. A boy was going to be suspended from wires in front of a standard green screen (which had already been rented), and the green screen process would make him look as though he was floating in space (much more on this in Chapter 7). I offhandedly mentioned that of course we would have to make sure the boy's wardrobe was appropriate for the work. We went to the wardrobe department, where the director showed me the loudest Hawaiian shirt I'd ever seen, with lots of green in it! Diplomatically, I explained that the green screen process would make the green areas on the shirt look like holes in the boy through which we would see space, and therefore it would be good to use a different shirt. The director was silent for a moment. Then he told me that the boy had been wearing that same shirt for the last twelve weeks of filming. We couldn't change it. And the **effects** work started the next day!

Obviously, we had a problem. We had little choice but to delay for a few days. First, I had the wardrobe department dye down the colors in the shirt, and we experimented to find the degree of muting that prevented them from triggering the process effect. Next, I designed a transition effect to blast the kid into space that would help to cover the change in his shirt's appearance. All this cost time and money, and the director (who was also the producer) was not pleased, but he had no choice. If only the requirements of Post had been considered during Prep, a simple wardrobe change would have saved literally thousands of dollars.

As technology has advanced, Post has assumed a larger and larger role in the creative life of films. Until recently, most of a show was shot during principal photography; now, much may be created only after the Shoot is over. With visual effects and computer-generated imagery (CGI) invading all aspects of film production, the distinction between Shoot and Post has diminished. People and processes that used to be thought of as belonging to the realm of Post, such as visual effects supervisors and CGI artists, are now being involved earlier and earlier in the production; conversely, directors, cinematographers, and editors are continuing to work actively all the way to delivery.

This change has been reflected in production budgets. The rule of thumb used to be that Post was about 10 percent of the total budget of a show. For a $10 million picture, for example, you would probably spend about $1 million on Post. For that amount, you could edit the picture, have the music composed and recorded, have the rest of the sound work done, complete the final mix, and produce the necessary prints for delivery of the film. (For a low-budget independent feature, Post may be one-third of the total budget because it contains so many fixed costs that cannot be reduced.) As technology has advanced and more and more creative work is done in Post, however, the proportion of costs has changed. In a big effects picture, Post can easily account for more than 40 percent of the total budget.

All this means that Prep must include detailed planning for both the Shoot *and* Post.

The Human Face of Post

As the computer has begun to play a larger and larger role in the production process, many people have started to worry that our films are losing some of their human quality. Sometimes, when I'm watching a movie that seems full of effects but devoid of a strong emotional core—a movie like *Armageddon* or *Independence Day,* for example—I find it easy to agree. But then I remind myself that overall, one thing is for sure: People make movies, not computers. As useful as computers may be in Post, no computer program will ever replace the eyes of the colorist, the ears of the **mixers,** and the storytelling instinct of the editors.

There is one unique quality that is shared by the people who work in Post. While directors and producers often talk of "vision," editors and the others who work in Post often talk about "revision." Editors especially must deal with the reality of what has been shot regardless of what was intended or written in the script. A quote that often shows up on editing room walls goes something like this: "Editors take unfocused, awkwardly composed, badly acted material and make it into a cohesive, graceful, and flowing story—for which the director takes the credit." Like most jokes, this one contains a grain of truth. The same might be said on behalf of the composers who strengthen emotion and drama, the sound editors who clean up and strengthen the dialogue, the sound designers who provide a sense of place and dramatic emphasis, the colorists who adjust the exposure and enrich the images, the effects editors who create whole sequences from scratch, and all the other specialists of Post who deal with the raw material supplied to them from the Shoot and bring it to its full potential, sometimes expanding or altering it to a significant degree. From the raw material of the dailies and production sound tracks, the people of Post find the diamonds in the rough, smooth them, and blend them with all the other elements in their arsenal to create a unified and lasting experience.

This must be kept in mind during Prep, when the key postproduction personnel are chosen. They must be dedicated people who have the technical skills, the artistic sensibility, and the collaborative temperament to recognize and align themselves with the particular vision that is driving the entire project. These key people, especially the editor, composer, sound supervisor, and postproduction supervisor, will in turn populate their departments with like-minded people, and so the necessary qualities will resonate throughout the far-flung postproduction organization.

The two other parts of this book, on editing and composing, discuss skills that depend a great deal on natural talent. As in most of the arts, there is something mysterious at the heart of both editing and composing that can't be taught and can't be learned from a book. But happily for many of us, the postproduction process *can* be described and learned by anyone of reasonable intelligence. Unlike editing and composing, there's not a lot of mystery here. All you need is the willingness to learn a little about technology and technical processes and a lot about people and then learn how to apply it to the assignment at hand.

The Postproduction Supervisor

When most people think of the personnel working in Post, they usually think first of the editor, who is indeed the most creatively influential member of the Post team. But a myriad of other people also have tremendous creative input, including the sound designers, sound editors, music editors, the many assistant editors, the colorists, and the mixers. In many "effects" movies, a primary creative role is played by the many kinds of special effects artists. The job of coordinating all these disparate and far-flung people falls to the postproduction supervisor. Even in low-budget independent or student filmmaking, in which there may not be a separate person called the postproduction supervisor, the coordination of Post processes must be overseen by someone, be it the **producer** or the director.

Post supervisors get many different credits in different kinds of movies and television shows. The person in charge of Post may be called the postproduction supervisor, the associate producer (especially in television), or the coproducer. The credits have become more and more confusing over the years and vary even within specific segments of the industry. We'll simply refer to the person in charge as the post production supervisor.

Robert Benedetti has described the job of the producer as being "a traffic cop at the intersection of art and commerce."[3] This is also true of the postproduction supervisor. There is often a conflict between the demands of art and the restrictions imposed by time and money. Wide knowledge, reliable information, and ingenuity are required to resolve that conflict so as to make creativity and high quality possible.

The postproduction supervisor should be an expert on the latest state-of-the-art technologies, as well as the old-fashioned ways of doing things. He or she needs up-to-the-minute information on the best deals and facilities in town, such as when to use one editing facility over another, where the best value for sound recording can be found, and where the best mixers are currently working. He or she is also expected to know enough about every aspect of the Post process to solve creatively and inexpensively any problems that arise or at least to know who can. The postproduction supervisor helps to hire a lot of people and make a lot of deals. It is a job of details.

It is useful for the postproduction supervisor to have an editorial background, but it is not essential. What *is* essential is an understanding of the temperament of creative people and what environment, systems, and materials they need to do their best work. I like to think of it as creating the best possible "play space." The job is to support the work of everyone on the team, to maintain the schedule and the budget, and most of all to preserve a sense of service to the script itself and the director's vision of the movie.

Coordination is certainly one of the most important aspects of the postproduction supervisor's job. He or she makes sure that in every department, the right people are in the right place at the right time, with the equipment and materials they need to do their jobs well, and that they are working in a coordinated way so that the various elements needed to finish the picture are ready on time. Once the train has left the station, the postproduction supervisor is the conductor that keeps it moving and reaching each of the many stations on time.

The supervisor has three main devices that he or she can use to keep everyone on schedule: the design of the process itself, the schedule, and the budget. Let's look at each.

Design of the Process

Figures 3.2, 4.1, and 5.1, on pages 27, 33, and 40, are flowcharts that describe the sequence of each step in various kinds of Post processes. I often work out such a chart for each of my projects. Making the chart forces me to think through every detail, even for a process I've been through hundreds of times before. (It's easy to take familiar things for granted.) Sometimes the flowchart will describe a given phase of a project, such as how we will produce dailies and get them on everyone's desk. Besides its value to me in thinking things through, the chart can be used to communicate to others. It helps the producers to understand what we are doing and helps the various departments to see how their work interrelates to the overall scheme of things.

[3]Robert Benedetti, *From Concept to Screen: An Overview of Film and Television Production,* Allyn & Bacon, 2002, p. 2.

Schedule

Schedules are ideal constructs, and they often have to change in the face of reality. I publish a revised schedule as often as necessary. On a television series, this usually means once a week; on a movie, perhaps only once a month. But everyone needs to be plugged into the schedule at all times.

Budget

I make it a point to create a lot of memos about the budget. The producers have the prerogative to make financial decisions, but they can't do it without the best financial information. If they are considering doing something that is going to add to the budget, they must have that information *before* they make their decision. The postproduction supervisor must be able to provide a reliable estimate of a potential cost at a moment's notice. (This also helps to avoid the syndrome in which the producer makes a decision, then sees the cost overrun and says to the supervisor, "Why didn't you warn me? Now you'll just have to find the money somewhere.")

The Postproduction Empire

On larger projects, the postproduction supervisor may be assisted by a postproduction coordinator whose job will be to oversee all communications within the far-flung Post empire. Whoever is responsible for coordination will create a contact list and perhaps even an organization chart, showing each of the people and vendors involved in the project. I like to put this list or chart on my office bulletin board; since most of the people who work in Post are at some distance from one another, it's easy to forget how many people are off-site at the editing suite, the sound studio, the optical house, the film laboratory, or the other out-of-house vendors.

The main categories of a Post contact list usually are as follows:

1. Post staff: the supervisor, coordinator, and PA (production assistant)
2. Production staff: director, producers of all kinds, director of photography (**DP**), production supervisor
3. Editorial staff: editor, assistants, apprentices, editing system supplier
4. Studio or network contacts: director of postproduction, creative executives, legal affairs officer
5. Accounting: postproduction accountant, payroll service
6. Courier services: courier, FedEx, etc.
7. Film lab and video dailies
8. Music: composer, music editor
9. **Negative cutter**
10. Sound: sound facility scheduler, sound supervisor, dubbing stage, ADR, loop group

11. Title and optical house
12. Video duplication
13. Visual effects suppliers
14. Miscellaneous

When you add them all up, there are usually between 40 and 150 people working in Post for even a modest film. On a big effects picture, we'll add CGI artists, model makers, motion capture specialists, creature creators, puppeteers, and so on. The number can rise to many hundreds of people. Just watch the end credits of a picture such as *Lord of the Rings: The Fellowship of the Ring.* It looks like the census of a small city!

2 The Post Budget

Outlandish stories of wild extravagances and budget overages of pictures like *Heaven's Gate, Waterworld,* or *Titanic* are so common that it is easy to conclude that movie budgets are only a joke. Nothing could be farther from the truth. Most projects are tightly budgeted and most producers, whose own financial return is at risk, control their budgets with an iron fist. As a result of careful planning and tracking, most films and TV shows hit their budgetary targets within a few percent.

This is not a matter of luck. It comes from working out the details, making good cost estimates, and—most of all—anticipating the problems. As a postproduction supervisor, my job is to develop the "B" plan. I'm constantly trying to figure out what might go wrong (which, according to Murphy's Law, will) and how I'm going to deal with it.

Creating the Budget

A budget doesn't spring fully born from the brow of Zeus. It evolves slowly through many phases. It begins with a preliminary estimate that is created as soon as a script is considered for production. This initial estimate, based on an estimated shooting schedule, is carefully considered by the financing entity in judging the feasibility of the project. If the project then receives the green light, a more detailed budgetary process begins and continues throughout Prep. The producer, line producer, and/or unit production manager (UPM) pore over every detail of the budget as deals are made and costs are estimated. The budget for Post is fully considered as part of this overall budgetary process.

As we plan the Post budget, we have to make some very basic choices. It is true that nowadays we can do very nearly anything in Post, given enough time and resources. The question is, what is the proper balance among the scope of the project, the available time, and the quality of the results desired? To help others understand this, I often draw a triangle that looks like the one in Figure 2.1. We try not to pick Cheap, but sometimes it is thrust on us. If we have to be Cheap, we know we'll need more time, because Good can be had for Cheap but not very Fast. Sometimes we are inspired and skillful and lucky, and we manage to do all three, but that's a rare blessing.

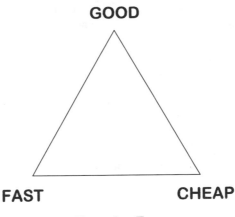

FIGURE 2.1   Choose Any Two.

During this planning process, we define everything we can, down to the last detail. Finally, we publish a proposed budget and the financing entity—be it a network, a cable company, a studio, or a group of independent financiers—examines it, and after much negotiation (during which the budget is usually reduced), it is approved. Once it is approved (or *locked*), everyone concerned actually signs the budget and pledges themselves to keeping it—the producers at the peril of reduced fees, the rest at the peril of their professional reputations. We never, never "wing it."

The Budget Form

Appendix A gives you an example of the many items in a typical film or television production budget. These are listed in the standard form, fairly common throughout the industry, created by a computer program such as *Movie Magic Budgeting*. The specific line items are created from a chart of accounts. Simply put, the chart of accounts is a standardized set of categories of potential costs. The major headings and the account numbers that are often assigned to them in production budgets are shown in Appendix A. The items listed are the main departments that would be shown on the summary page of a budget, called the *top sheet;* in the many detail pages that accompany the summary, there are many subaccounts within each of these headings.

You will notice that the overall budget is divided into two large groups of items, those that are **above-the-line,** and those that are **below-the-line.** The "line" is an accounting term. Below-the-line costs are relatively stable given the nature of a specific production; here people are paid on a weekly basis according to established union rates, equipment is rented according to customary rates, and so on. Above-the-line costs, however, are not so easy to predict, since they are set by individual negotiation and can vary widely. In particular, the same film shot in the same length of time can cost millions of dollars more or less depending on the fees negotiated for the story, director, and stars and the commensurate costs generated by the presence of stars, who are very high-maintenance people.

Different types of production have different charts of accounts adapted to their specific needs. The account for editors, for example, might apply, in different situations, to picture editors, trailer editors, sound editors, and music editors. Currently, my firm is involved with a TV series in China, a miniseries in Prague, a reality show on the road, and a concert tour in Europe. Each one requires a different kind of budget, but working with a basic chart of accounts, we are easily able to craft budgets to meet the different requirements of each project. Working from a basic chart of accounts helps to ensure that necessary costs are not overlooked.

Doing a Budget Breakdown

In the case of network, cable, or studio projects, the budget-making process is governed by clearly established procedures, principles, and forms. In the independent world, the financing entity, be it a group of investors or even the filmmakers themselves, deserves to see a carefully considered budgetary projection. In both cases, the creation of the budget follows roughly the same process, though the amounts and categories involved may be different.

The golden rule throughout the budget-making process is "Go slow and be specific." Decisions and estimates made now will spell the difference between heaven and hell for weeks and months to come. Overlooked items will always come back to haunt you.

The budget-making process begins with a careful **breakdown** of the script. I begin the breakdown by simply reading the script with an open mind, with not so much as a pencil in my hand. This is probably the last time for quite a while that I'll have the opportunity to actually enjoy the script for its own sake. I let my mind run free and visualize characters, effects, music, and sound. I gently store these impressions; then I go back to the top, pick up pencil and paper, and begin work on a detailed breakdown.

My first pass notes anything that sticks out for any reason: special production problems such as fire or water sequences, specific mentions of source music or products that might need clearances and the payment of royalties, anything that might require CGI or other special visual effects or models, and so on.

On the second pass, it starts to get tricky as the details begin to accumulate. There are four things that must be considered when planning every aspect of the Post budget: people (personnel and vendors), schedule, budget, and processes. My notes are getting thick and detailed.

On the basis of this preliminary breakdown I can now begin to ask some basic questions. I usually start at the end of the Post process and work backwards, considering first the eventual form of delivery required for the finished film. When is the final project due? Will it be finished on film, with all the special processes required, such as cutting negatives, timing, and printing? Or is it to be delivered on video, in which case a whole different set of processes will be required? The *finishing,* the portion of the work that begins after the final mix, will affect the budget tremendously, and I need to know the specifics of the delivery requirements.

There may be special considerations that are unique to a given project that will add cost. It is surprising how often studios and networks neglect to inform a producer of these, so I always ask: Are there special screenings before release that will require early videos or prints, with temp sound tracks? What are the requirements of publicity, and how will trailers and promos be created? What are these intermediate deadlines? I learned this the hard way when I was nearing the completion of a film and was suddenly informed that we had about a week to create a presentation for the studio boss to show at a meeting of the board of directors. We stopped everything and hurriedly compiled a piece from selected scenes and about fifteen of our best visual effects, jammed some music under it, and finished mixing the night before it was due, almost missing the last plane that could deliver it to the meeting. After all that, the studio had the gall to complain that I ended up over budget by the $50,000 the piece had cost to produce. Who knew?

Working backwards from the delivery, I then consider the needs of the final mix, the sound work, the music composing and recording, the staffing and equipping of the editorial department, the processing and delivery of **dailies.** Again, my four topics— people, schedule, budget, and process—are considered in each area. The schedules for special effects, music, sound, credits and titles, **opticals,** additional photography, and so on, are considered in detail to be sure that each component will be ready when needed. In this sense, a film is like constructing a building: The framing has to follow the foundation, the electrical and plumbing have to go in after the framing but before the plasterboard, and so on. If any one of the many needed elements is not ready on time, the whole process will grind to a halt, and the budget will dissolve into chaos.

Finally, the matter of a **contingency** must be considered. Prudence suggests that it is a good idea to have a little money set aside for unforeseen expenses; and many networks, studios, and bonding companies (who provide a **guarantee** that the needed funds will be available as long as the project is completed on schedule and budget) absolutely require contingencies, usually 10 percent of the total budget. This, however, takes needed money away from other departments; the correct impulse of every good budgeter is to try to get as much of the money "up on the screen" as possible, and costs that don't contribute to the quality of the finished product—such as the contingency— are to be avoided. Besides, the existence of a contingency may encourage a lack of discipline. And what do we do with the money if we don't spend it? It can be a sneaky way for a network or studio to reduce its costs.

Working within the Budget

Now our Post budget is locked, and everyone has signed off on it. The picture begins to shoot; dailies are rolling in. Editing has begun, and already many Post processes are gearing up. Things begin to happen very fast and sometimes very big, and costs can change just as fast and just as big. Not surprisingly, costs are tracked on a daily basis, with **hot cost** reports (which show items that are deviating from the estimates) and extensive weekly **cost reports.** These all-important reports are prepared by the production accountants, the people sitting endlessly in front of computers, who are responsible for keeping track of every penny spent and alerting the producers when it looks as though anything might be going wrong. Later, after the picture **wraps,** one of these people will usually continue as our Post accountant.

Now and then, things go awry. Costs depend on a number of factors, and perhaps the most influential is the alignment and harmony at the top of the production team. My wife is a production accountant (we met on a production, which will give you an idea how far I'll go to keep a show on budget). She is convinced that whenever the producers and the director are on the same page, the show makes its budget, but when they are at odds, the overages start. In my experience, she's right.

Another reason for overages is that some costs simply cannot be accurately predicted. One of my early jobs was on a TV show called *Max Headroom,* the very first to use a computer-altered main character. We were constantly breaking new technological ground and had no precedents on which we could base our budget estimates. Costs soared. Our only excuse was that, in a real sense, we were doing research and development for the entire television medium.

At other times, unforeseen events beyond anyone's control (what the lawyers call *force majeur*) will affect costs. When I was working at Lorimar years ago, an actor was injured on one of my shows, and production had to be shut down for a few weeks; our schedule and budget were out the window, and I was sick with worry. Lorimar's Vice President of Postproduction, a wonderful, Pattonesque gentlemen named Chuck Silvers, handed me a form to fill out, itemizing all of the things that would be affected by the shutdown. "Don't worry," he explained, "it's an approved overage." The idea of an "approved overage" always seemed to me like an oxymoron, but it really does make sense. When the budget was locked, each individual item in the budget was also locked; savings in one area are not automatically available to offset an overage in another. This prevents wily producers from hiding any padding in various nooks and crannies of the budget. It also prevents the dangerous attitude that it will be okay to spend more in one area because we "can make it up" in some other—thinking that leads inevitably to an overrun in the bottom line. Nor is the contingency—if there is one—readily available for this kind of eventuality, since networks and studios like to think of the contingency as "their" money.

Therefore, as production moves along, every cost that was not anticipated—and I do mean *every*—is discussed, and the producers must seek specific approval for that item. If the additional cost is deemed necessary or acceptable, an approval is given, and this is an "approved overage." The executives who oversee production budgets can sometimes be extremely difficult about giving these approvals, but if the bottom line is on track, there is usually a little give and take in specific areas.

From all this, you can see that budgets are a serious and complex matter. Time is money, we say, but in filmmaking, it is more true to say that money is time and people and space and the opportunity for creativity.

CHAPTER

3

Working with Film

It is theoretically possible that by the time this book is in your hands, this entire chapter will be obsolete. In 2002, *Star Wars, Episode II* became the first large-scale live action film to be a purely digital product. Of course, some much more modest live-action films have also been shot in digital in recent years, such as *Timecode, The Celebration, The Buena Vista Social Club,* and *The Blair Witch Project.* Several major animated films have been created by entirely digital means as well, such as 2001's *Shrek* and *Monsters, Inc.* However, because so few theaters are equipped for digital projection these films have been "finished in film," that is, laser printed from digital to film for distribution (although they were also projected digitally in those few digitally equipped theaters; *Star Wars, Episode II* was shown digitally in only about twenty theaters nationwide).

Despite the small number of theaters equipped for digital projection, however, the need for film is diminishing. There are plans to equip more than 200 theaters with digital projection systems within the next two years, though it remains to be seen whether these plans will be realized as quickly as George Lucas and others hope. There are several obstacles. First, several major theater chains, which expanded too fast during the economic boom of the 1990s, have recently filed for bankruptcy, and the building of new theaters has slowed dramatically. Second, the lack of industry-wide digital standards has slowed the adoption of digital presentations in theaters. Third, and most important, there is the high cost of converting theaters from film to video projection systems, currently about $500,000 per screen. The studios expect the theater owners (exhibitors) to bear the cost of the conversion, but the exhibitors argue that since digital will save the studios the $2 billion or so they currently spend annually on prints and shipping, the studios should bear the cost. The argument rages on, but there are predictions that by 2010, half the movies shown in U.S. theaters will be projected digitally. Certainly, pioneers like George Lucas hope that *Star Wars, Episode II* will encourage this revolution.

Even after digital projection becomes common, however, there will still be some filmmakers who will insist on using good, old-fashioned film. Film will survive for other uses, as well. For example, film has the longest archival permanence, whereas digital images must be renewed every decade or so. Films that were originally exposed at the turn of the last century are still viewable, albeit just barely. (We will have more to say on the archival use of film in Chapter 9.)

Finally, it is unclear whether other parts of the world will switch to digital as quickly and completely as the United States hopes to. Film will probably be the only truly international standard for a long time to come. 35mm film is shown throughout the world, and despite many different formats, any basic projector can at least put the image on the screen, and in most cases, today's equipment can show any film made since 1920 or so. Try that with the videotape formats of more than fifteen years ago, or try showing a European PAL tape on an American NTSC VCR!

For all these reasons, we will begin our examination of Post processes by describing the best ways of working with film. The marketplace will decide if and when this time-honored medium is to be relegated to the technology museum, but for now, we will begin by describing a film-only process. As we do, keep in mind that nowadays, almost everyone uses a mixture of film and video technologies. Video, for example, has almost entirely replaced film for use as dailies and in editing. But we'll cover the video processes later and for now stick with those few diehards, like Steven Spielberg's editor Michael Kahn, who insist on editing on film, even movies as complex as *Jurassic Park* and *Saving Private Ryan.*

Film Sizes and Formats

An important difference between film and video is the shape of the frame itself. This proportion of frame height to width is called the **aspect ratio.** When Thomas Edison developed his camera, he chose a frame that was three units high by four units wide ("3 by 4"). This can be expressed numerically as 1.33:1 (one-third wider than high). Edison's aspect ratio became the standard for all films until 1952, when the short-lived three-camera/three-projector format called Cinerama appeared. A more lasting change was signaled in 1953, when 20th Century Fox brought out the biblical epic *The Robe* in CinemaScope. Other wide-screen formats soon followed. The use of stereophonic sound, which had been introduced in 1940 by Disney's *Fantasia,* also became standard.

CinemaScope remains the widest aspect ratio in use today at 2.35:1 (two and one-third times wider than high), although most feature films are shot in more moderately wide-screen formats, either the Standard Academy ratio of 1.85:1, or the Foreign Theatrical standard of 1.66:1. Wide-screen formats require a special type of lens on both camera and projector that permits the wide image to be compressed onto a normal film frame, then uncompressed when projected; these formats are called **anamorphic.** Edison's old ratio of 1.33:1, however, remains the standard for ordinary broadcast television (Figure 3.1).

The advanced digital video systems used for motion pictures today (often called high-definition video, or simply HD) are also wide-screen but use a unique aspect ratio of 1.78:1 (three-fourths wider than it is high), which is also called "16 by 9." It is third on the list in Figure 3.1.

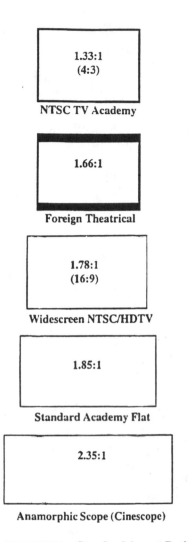

FIGURE 3.1   Standard Aspect Ratios.

Film stock itself is named according to its width. Curiously, Eastman Kodak, an American Company, was the first to adopt the new international standard of metric measurement at the beginning of the 20th Century. George Eastman, the inventor of motion picture film, was a true visionary and realized that film had a very international market (as does Kodak itself, its name being pronounced the same way in every language on the planet). Film is unique in this regard among U.S. consumer products; we speak easily of 35mm film, but we still "pick up a quart of milk."

35mm is the most common size of film stock in the U.S. entertainment industry, although 16mm is the most-used film stock globally. There is also 70mm film, but there hasn't been a film shot in that large format since Kenneth Branagh's *Hamlet* in 1996 and Tom Cruise's *Far and Away* before that in 1992. (A few prints of some films, such as *Lord of the Rings,* are enlarged to 70mm and shown on a very few large-format screens in major cities.) Besides 16mm, 35mm, and 70mm, there are a few special formats. The most familiar of these is IMAX. This is a special 65mm film that, unlike any other film stock, is shot and projected horizontally. It can be shown only in special IMAX-equipped theaters. (IMAX has recently developed a process to transfer certain feature films to IMAX film for showing in its theaters; Disney's *Beauty and the Beast* was the first.)

The film stock that is used in motion pictures is almost always a negative stock; that is, when the image is developed after being shot, it is a negative image, with whites rendered as blacks and colors rendered as their complements. (There are also films that produce a positive image, called *reversal* stocks, but they are by and large obsolete.) Shooting in negative allows for considerable control in the final printing of the movie; color and exposure can be corrected and blended. Also, there are a number of special film processes, such as prefogging (exposing the film to a small amount of light before shooting to mute and enrich its color quality) and special bleaching processes, such as the one used in *Black Hawk Down.* These special processes are available only when creating prints from a film negative, although they can be mimicked by digital processes.

Double-System Sound and Synchronization

The negative that is shot in the film camera does not contain the sound being recorded. Sound is recorded on a tape or digital recorder that is often some distance from the camera. This procedure is commonly referred to as **double-system** sound recording. Double-system recording has several advantages. For instance, multiple cameras are sometimes run simultaneously during filming. The double system allows these cameras to operate independently and all then share the common **soundtrack.** Most important, the quality of the recorded sound is greatly improved, since it can be recorded on much better systems and materials than would be available from recording mechanisms within the film camera. This is so important that all forms of professional production, including video, use double-system sound recording. In even the lowest-budget production, the importance of sound quality is a necessity.

The main difficulty created by double-system recording is **synchronization,** keeping the picture and sound perfectly related to one another. If the speed of the recording device isn't exactly related to the speed of the film, the synchronization will be lost. Imagine, for example, riding on an escalator; your hand is on the black handrail, but because the handrail is moving just a bit faster than the stairs themselves, your hand gradually drifts ahead of your feet—you go "out of sync."

Two systems are in common use to keep the film in the camera and the tape on the recorder in perfect sync: the **control track** and the **time code.** The control track is simply a 60-Hz signal (the same frequency as the electric current in your house) that is recorded on the tape alongside the production soundtrack. During playback, this control track is played by a second machine that keeps the recording at its exact original speed by "resolving" the 60-Hz tone to its original pitch. If the speed of the original recorder varied for any reason (perhaps the batteries were losing power), the resolver in the playback machine makes sure that the original speed is sensed and compensated for—quite simple, quite clever.

Now that we have the sound traveling at the right speed, we have to establish the exact place to start the tape in relation to the picture. This is called the **sync point.** This is created by the famous **clapperboard** used at the beginning of each shot. The board, or **slate** (it was once a small chalkboard), identifies the **shot, take,** and other critical information. On top of the slate is a *clapstick* that can be banged down onto the top of the slate. The assistant editor simply finds the exact frame where the clapstick closes, then finds the sound of the clap on the audio track, moves them together, and sync is established.

Nowadays, we usually use an electronic slate called a *"SmartSlate"* instead of a clapper. This is a board that contains a rapidly changing digital display that freezes on the time code (see below) when the camera assistant closes the clapper. Later, at the film laboratory, the developed film is transferred to video through the process called **telecine,** the term for any process that converts light into electrical data. (This was once done by simply projecting the film into a video camera, but today it is done by scanning the negative with a laser.) The telecine operator simply reads the time code displayed on the slate and types the code into the audio playback machine, which goes automatically to the sync point. There are also now some film cameras, such as the Aaton, that lay down time code as they shoot, enabling synchronization in a similar way.

Time Code

It isn't enough to depend entirely on the control track and sync points. The slate establishes the start point, but you also need a way of finding the sync frame within the huge volume of film that was shot. Even though each film frame is numbered on its edge, these edge numbers cannot be used until they are correlated to the actual picture. This is accomplished by creating a **video time code** at the time the dailies are transferred from the negative to video by telecine. This is simply a code that records the running time of the developed film in hours, minutes, seconds, and frames. If the dailies come from the first day of shooting, the hour is 1; the dailies for the second day of shooting begin with hour 2, and so on. The sync point of a particular scene might occur at 3:22:05:09, and this point can be correlated with the specific frame number on the film. All three of these reference codes—the audio time code, the video time code, and the frame numbers—are printed in windows on the dailies, as shown in Figure 11.3 on page 77.

Because there is no such thing as absolute time (so says Einstein), the time code can drift slightly. Your wristwatch drifts, your computer clock drifts, the atomic clock in Greenwich drifts (although not as much as your wristwatch). This drift is not a problem over a short period of time, as in a thirty-second commercial, but in a one-hour drama, the time code can be off by as much as four seconds. The time code therefore needs to be adjusted periodically. To deal with this, the Society of Motion Picture Arts and Sciences (**SMPTE**) created two types of time code: **drop frame** and **non-drop frame.** Non-drop frame time code cannot be adjusted and is used for commercials and anywhere else where accurate time is not critical (dailies, nonbroadcast tapes, and so on). Drop Frame time code is much more accurate, generally within two frames or so at any given moment. As the name implies, it works by dropping (skipping) two frames at the top of every minute. If you are working with drop frame time code, you might notice a few numbers missing in the audio time code window, though the images will not be affected.

The Film Process

Now that we have established synchronization with the soundtrack, we must print and edit the film, create and incorporate any special visual effects, incorporate the music and sound tracks, and finally prepare the negatives from which we can make many pristine prints for distribution to theaters. Look at Figure 3.2. It is a flowchart showing the steps of the process that goes from a film origination (a film shoot) to a film finish.

Let's trace this process step by step. The original camera negative is sent to the film laboratory, where everything that was exposed is carefully processed. After processing, the camera negative is carefully examined and separated into **A negative** (or A neg) and **B negative** (or B neg), which are industry slang terms for the takes the director has asked to have printed (the A neg) and the rejected takes (the B neg). The B neg is saved in case it is needed later, but it is not included with the dailies. (Don't be confused by the terms "B neg" and "B roll." **B roll** is the general term for cutaways and other shots that are not the central focus of the scene. The term "B roll" is also used by the video crews who shoot material on the set of the film for use in the promotional material called the EPK, the electronic press kit. For them, interview footage shot with a star or director is separated from "B roll" footage shot on the set during filming.)

Assuming that the picture is being edited in film (a rare occurrence nowadays), the A neg must now be printed onto positive film stock to create the dailies. This printing is usually done at a single standard exposure and produces what we call *one-light* dailies. The DP (director of photography) sometimes establishes this exposure setting to approximate the desired look of the finished film. In very rare cases, the exposure for each shot on the dailies may be separately adjusted or timed, but this is an expensive luxury, since the entire film will be timed again after it is edited.

When film dailies are printed, they must be synchronized with a separate strip containing the sound recorded on the set. The finished dailies are then simultaneously delivered to the director, to the producers and executives supervising the production, and to the editing room. In the editing room, the dailies are broken down and organized

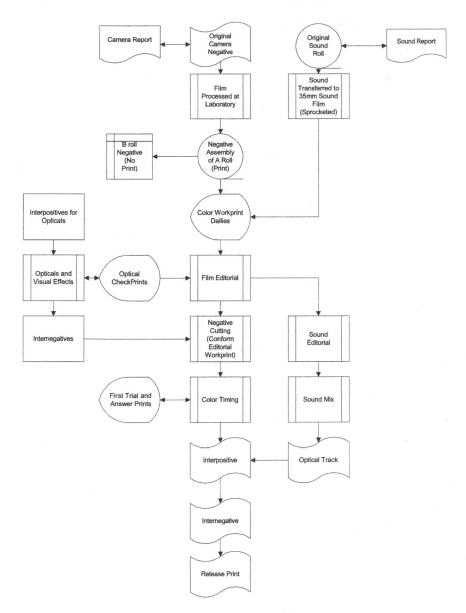

FIGURE 3.2   The Steps from Film Shoot to Film Finish.

by the assistant editor so that they will be ready for the editor to begin work. These organized dailies are now called the **workprint.** This workprint will be run through the editing machine (the sound strip is run simultaneously with the film) again and again. Sometimes a reprint will have to be ordered if the workprint gets too dirty or scratched.

Videotape and Digital Dailies

Except for those few editors who continue to cut on film, most productions now use videotape dailies. In this process, the takes that the director selects (the A negative) are developed and transferred directly to video without being printed. This is accomplished, as was explained earlier, by the telecine process. During telecine, the sound is synchronized electronically directly from the original recording, usually by the SmartSlate system described earlier or by time code originated in the camera.

Videotape dailies have several advantages over film. In film, dailies must be put into a projector to be viewed. The image is much better than on video, and the DP might want to see the earliest work on film to check his or her exposures, but for most purposes, film dailies are much too expensive and cumbersome. Videotape dailies are much easier and cheaper to produce, ship, and view. One thing has been lost, however. In the days of film dailies, everyone on the creative team would gather in the projection room and watch the dailies together. Now, with tape dailies, we go our separate ways, to our trailers, offices, and homes, and have become removed from each other. Notes fly back and forth after the dailies are viewed, but like all indirect communication, there is a greater chance of misunderstanding and a loss of personal nuance and less chance of truly creative collaboration and enthusiasm. Everything is a tradeoff.

The videotape dailies created in telecine are sent to the editing room, where they are "digitized" into electronic files in the editing computer. Along with the picture and sound, the files also include the metadata (also called the *flex file*). Metadata (meaning "data about data") refers to the information that must accompany the picture itself to render it useful. The metadata includes the film and video time codes and (if the show was shot on film) the film frame numbers, as well as scene and take information. All this goes into the computer, both to guide the editor in his or her work and to allow for technical lists to be generated at the end of the editorial process.

Videotape dailies are themselves quickly becoming obsolete in favor of digital dailies. Digitized dailies can be transmitted over special phone lines, inserted directly into the editing system together with their metadata, then discussed and manipulated in real time by editors, directors, and producers who may not even be in the same city. Several systems have been developed to handle this process, such as the Picture Pipeline system used by *The Third Watch*.

Opticals and Special Visual Effects

As early in the project as possible, the director and the editor try to identify all the shots that need any form of special treatment, as well as any special visual effects that must be created and inserted later. This work takes considerable time in film, and it is wise to get to it early. These sections are sent out to an *optical house* or a *special effects house*. At these facilities, the needed pieces of original camera negative are printed again onto special film stock to create an **interpositive.** Attention is paid to make the interpositive an accurate representation of the negative. After checking, the interpositive is reprinted through a machine called an **optical printer** (hence the term "opticals"). As the effect is created in the optical printer, it is photographed again as an **internegative.** This negative is printed conventionally and, if approved, is sent back to editorial, where it is cut into the movie.

The optical printer provides detailed computer control to allow the operator to crop, pan, twist, and otherwise manipulate the image. By photographing several passes onto the new film, multiple images—from simple **dissolves** to complex fantasy scenes—are created. (We'll deal in more detail with visual effects in Chapter 7.)

Cutting the Negative and Printing

The few editors who still cut in film, using the old-fashioned **movieola** or a **flatbed** editing machine such as the Steenbeck, actually **splice** every cut in the film by hand as they create the workprint. As tedious and slow as this sounds, those who work this way are amazingly fast and claim that this manual process has a rhythm that produces a more thoughtful product than does electronic editing (though many who work electronically would dispute this).

In any case, once the workprint is finished or "locked," the original negatives must be prepared for printing. The final version of the workprint is sent to the negative cutter, who carefully matches the frame numbers on the edge of the workprint with those on the original camera negative, cut by cut. The negatives are then arranged on **A and B rolls** (yet another use of these confusing terms). This permits the film to be printed with seamless cuts as the image switches from one roll to another with no intervening splice. The painstaking work of negative cutting must be done in a dust-free environment, and mistakes made here are irretrievable.

The negative will not be cut until the last possible moment, since even a locked cut might be "opened" to make last-minute changes. In fact, if there is enough time, it is always best to wait until the film has been mixed on the dubbing stage and played back for the director and the producer before giving the final okay to cut negative. But if time is short (as it often is), the negative will be cut while the final sound work is being done.

The cut negative is then timed: The exposure times in the printer are adjusted to change the brightness and color balance cut by cut to achieve a uniform look. This is done by a specialist called (you guessed it) a **timer** or colorist, under the supervision of the DP or sometimes the postproduction supervisor and sometimes even the director. The timing of the negative is a matter of considerable importance, since it establishes the look of the film. Once the timing settings are established, **trial prints** are made and examined, and adjustments are made if needed. When the final timing is approved, the print is referred to as the **answer print.**

Now it is time to create the many release prints. If the original negative were to be used for this purpose, it would soon wear out; in fact, running the original negative through the printer must be avoided because every pass could result in an irreparable scratch or tear. Instead, the cut negative is printed just one more time, using the settings established by the timing, onto reversal stock to create an interpositive, or **IP.** The IP is then used to print an internegative, or **IN.** Figure 3.3 shows the steps by which film alternates between negative and positive throughout the production process.

When the sound work is complete and has been mixed down, it is laid onto the IN as an **optical sound track.** In made-for-television movies, often called **MOWs** or "Movies of the week," and television series and with some theatrical films, however, optical tracks are no longer produced; instead, the final mixed track of the dub is transferred to a magnetic master tape, a **CD,** or any one of several new formats and projected in perfect sync with the film for a dual-system screening.

Many copies of the IN, called the "dupe negatives," are in turn used to print, often at incredible speeds, the many **release prints** that are sent to the theaters. Thousands of release prints can be created and shipped in a matter of days, and they often arrive with little time to spare before their first general release screenings. Quality control over release prints is a special concern; the dupe negatives wear out quickly, and new ones must be made from the IP. During all this, the precious original negative is stored, safe from wear and tear.

Dirt

There is much to criticize in this film-finishing process. Film dailies are bulky, film cutting is slow, the cost of printing and reprinting dailies is considerable, and preparing negative cut lists manually is tedious. There is one further problem with film stock: My mentor, Chuck Silvers, who was Vice President of Postproduction at Lorimar, Universal, Columbia, and MGM during his career, once said to me, "The one thing that will eventually kill film is *dirt.*" As the film stock moves through a printer, editing machine, or projector, it naturally generates an electrical field that attracts all sorts of foreign materials, mostly lint and dust. Kodak has spent millions to develop a process that will keep film clean, but stuff still shows up on film. Like most filmmakers, I have chased scratches, static charges, and even errant staples that have shown up in the middle of my movies. At these times, I sometimes curse film stock as arcane and obsolete and think, "There's no dirt in digital" (although there are rare electronic quirks called **artifacts**).

When I'm feeling this way, however, I remember the work of all the filmmakers who preceded me. As I look at the bulky film cameras with their heavy magazines, the huge optical printers looking like something out of Flash Gordon, and the smelly vats of the film processors, I am reminded that these "obsolete" and "crude" devices created the worlds that made me want to become a filmmaker in the first place. They made true magic long before I came along, not because of snappy digital technology, but because those craftsmen knew how to use their tools to create art. As we move into the modern technology of digital filmmaking, I hope we remember that all the best tools in the world will not make a bad film great, and the best moments in film are often the simplest.

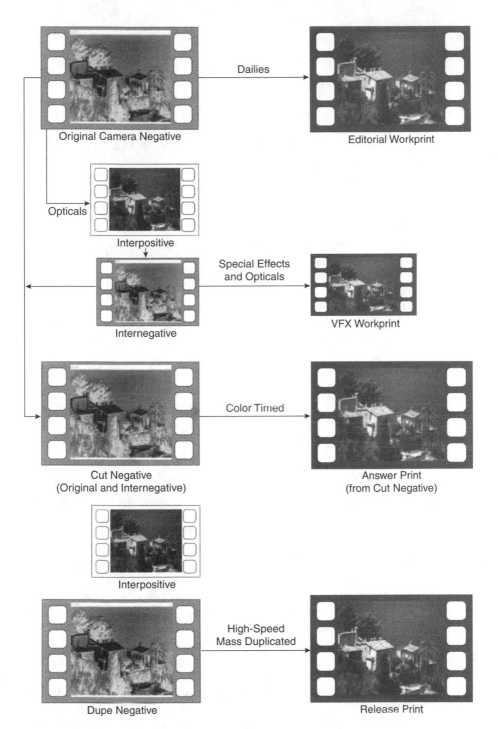

FIGURE 3.3   The Flow of Negative to Positive Film.

CHAPTER

4

The Nature of Video

Now that we understand the old-fashioned, tried-and-true process of working with film, let's take a look at the latest electronic techniques.

In actual practice, most of today's films utilize a mixture of film and video. The most common approach in feature films, television movies, sitcoms, and single-camera one-hour programs today, is to shoot on film, then transfer to video for the postproduction process. There are several reasons why film origination persists in these cases; film stock has much higher resolution than even the best video, providing a more versatile original source. Also, to many, the film image looks richer in quality than video, perhaps because the grains of film emulsion are distributed randomly, whereas the pixels of the video image are arranged on a strict grid. Finally, film can tolerate greater ranges of light and dark—that is, contrast—than video. It is often said by directors of photography who have worked in both mediums that you "light film" and "un-light video" because video can require substantially less light than film. It is an entirely new medium with its own properties and its own way of reacting to light, but a good cinematographer can adapt almost immediately to the difference.

As we described in Chapter 3, in those cases in which the original is shot in film, the exposed negative film is developed and transferred to videotape immediately, and editing is then done electronically. In the case of commercials, corporate and educational shows, and television sitcoms and episodic shows, the product is then finished, delivered, and broadcast in video as well, so in these cases, film has been abandoned except for shooting. The most common Post process in the industry today, therefore, is a film shoot to video finish.

However, for all theatrical feature films and TV movies that are to be released in theaters overseas, delivery must still be on film stock. After these shows have been edited, the electronic editing machine prints out instructions listing the film frame numbers for every cut, and the original film negatives are cut and printed just as described in the previous chapter. This is film shoot to video edit to film finish. Both these processes are described in Figure 4.1.

As video technology has developed, video is being used more and more throughout the entire process, from origination to finish. This is video shoot to video finish, and is the fulfillment of the video revolution. To understand it fully, let's start by examining the various qualities of video.

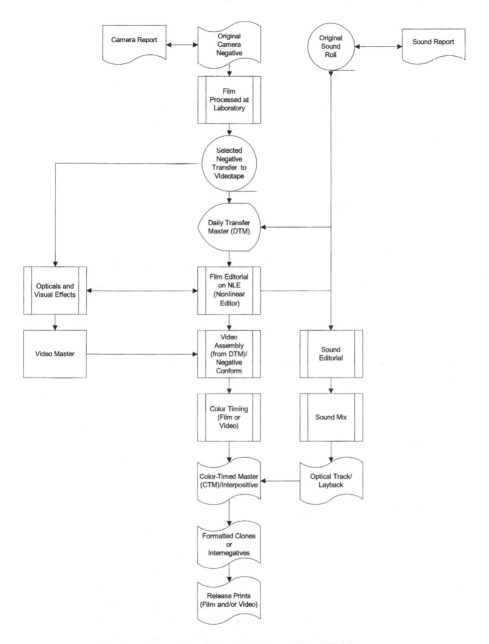

FIGURE 4.1   The Steps from Film Shoot to Film or Video Finish.

Analog and Digital

Most nontechnical people do not really know the difference between **analog** and **digital** television, but since this is becoming increasingly important, let's define the difference.

   Analog comes from the word "analogous," which is from the Latin meaning "like" or "similar to." This implies a certain lack of exactness, and analog information does indeed have this quality. An analog clock, for example, has hands that move continuously. You can see the moment at which the hands line up at noon, but it would be impossible to pin it down with complete accuracy (just as, in physics, the exact location of a swinging pendulum at any moment is only a probability). The electronic version of the moving hands of a digital clock is an electrical current with flowing modulations in its frequency or amplitude (as in FM or AM radio). The problem with analog systems is that they are not very good at recreating exactly the same phenomenon twice. You can experience this by drawing a squiggly line on a piece of paper and then trying to draw the same line again. No matter your skill, your copy is never going to be exactly the same as the original; it will be analogous or similar to the first line but not identical.

   Digital systems take a very different approach. If you draw a very fine grid over your squiggly line, you can see how the horizontal and vertical lines of the grid begin to turn your line into a series of fixed points. We can begin to recreate the line by recreating each little box. (Sign painters and muralists use this technique to make big versions of little drawings.) You can see that the more lines there are in the grid, the more little boxes, the better the definition (or **resolution**) of your line becomes. If you look at a digital TV image under a magnifier, you will see the little boxes; they are called **pixels** (which is how the digital production house Pixar got its name). The pixels are various colors, but each is a single, unitary piece of information (like 1 or 0, "on" or "off"). This is the digital image, capable of infinite and exact reproduction with no degradation between **generations,** every copy identical to the original.

Compression, Frames, and Streaming

Lately, the issues of **compression** and **streaming video** have been introduced into the world of Post. Let's try to sort them out. *Compression* means to stuff or squeeze something into a smaller space. If you stored all of the information your eye can register in 1/24th of a second (the duration of one film frame), you would have a computer file of about 40 megabytes (that's about ten times bigger than the computer file that stores the text for this book). By reducing the resolution of this image, we could compress the size of the file down to a more manageable size. A film frame holds about 12 megabytes of data. A frame of the best HDTV holds about 3 megabytes. An ordinary NTSC frame is about 1 megabyte or less. Unfortunately, compressing the image by reducing its level of resolution is a one-way street; we can't then restore its resolution because the data that provided that resolution has been lost. If you buy a VHS tape of an HDTV movie, it will never again look like HDTV, even on an HD set.

A better way of compressing the video image is by eliminating the idea of separate frames altogether and focusing instead only on the elements within the frame that change from moment to moment. If we are watching a static shot of a person in a room talking, for example, the wallpaper behind the person isn't moving. If we take a single frame and compare it to the frame before it and the frame after it, we can see that only a few things have changed, such as the person's lips. Why bother to recreate the entire frame when we can isolate only the things that change and move only those items into the next frame? This, in essence, is streaming video. The computer analyzes the picture with algorithms that understand the changing dynamics of the stream without bothering to recreate every frame. Only the piece of the frame that changes is stored, thus creating a much smaller file for the entire sequence. This results in compression with no loss of resolution.

Progressive and Interlaced Video

Today's broadcast television is displayed by using an archaic technique called **interlaced video.** This is because television technology is basically more than seventy years old. Early television experimenters had considerable problems in making the scan lines draw neatly together close enough to make a discernable image. Therefore, the creators of broadcasting designed a video frame that in fact is composed of two **fields.** Each of these fields contains one-half of the frame. The first field contains the odd lines of the frame (1, 3, 5, and so on), and the second field contains the even lines. When the frame is broadcast, the fields are interlaced together. In other words, all the odd lines are broadcast first, then one-thirtieth of a second later, all the even lines are broadcast. Thanks to the persistence of vision (the same phenomenon that makes movies work), you see it as one image. This is a messy system, and we could do much better, but the costs of changing the television broadcast system would be enormous (some estimate the cost to be more than $35 billion).

When computer manufacturers began to make their color monitors, however, they put together a different approach, called **progressive video.** This keeps all of the lines that make up the frame in one place and broadcasts (or scans) them consecutively (1, 2, 3, 4, and so on). The result is a much crisper image, which more closely emulates the look of film. Thus, the "p" in "24pHDTV" stands for "progressive." It substantially helps the new high-definition video to emulate film.

Video Standards and Resolution

It would be nice if there were a single standard for video, as there is for film, but there is not. Film is an international standard (thanks to Kodak), but video has several standards. There are four worth knowing about: NTSC, PAL, SECAM and HDTV.

In the minds of most people, the main difference between these standards is the matter of resolution, the sharpness of the image, which is mainly a function of the quantity of information contained within each frame. American NTSC television has 525 scan lines per frame. British PAL television has 625 lines, as does SECAM. The new HDTV standard has 1,080 lines of resolution. For comparison, 35mm film resolution is the equivalent of at least 2,500 lines per frame. Clearly, then, film has more "resolution" than even the best video, enabling it to photograph considerably more detail, and it will be a few years before we see these numbers change, though I predict that there will soon be a new high-resolution video format that will be even closer to the resolution of film; some such formats already exist in top-secret defense systems. Here is some background about each standard.

NTSC (National Television Standards Committee) is the standard in the United States, Canada, Mexico, and Japan. It broadcasts at the rate of 30 frames per seconds (fps), not 24 as in film. The discrepancy between NTSC video and film frame rates was ignored in the beginning; the Committee, meeting more than seventy years ago, simply never imagined that we would use video to make movies or even show films on television. As a result, NTSC video requires complicated conversion methods to transfer between 24-fps films and 30-fps video, a process called a **3:2 pulldown,** in which every other film frame is held for three video fields. This was, for many years, a real obstacle to shooting in video (although, as you will see, this obstacle has recently been overcome). How did the committee arrive at this nonsensical 30 fps, you might ask? For two reasons: First, they simply took the frequency of our electric current (60 cycles) and divided it by 2 to get 30 fps. They also experimented and found that this frame rate was the slowest that would render sports action in video without stuttering (sports were even then considered an important use of television). The NTSC image on your TV has 525 lines scanning horizontally across the screen in every frame, each divided into two fields that are interlaced together, thus allowing the frame to be refreshed twice as fast as if there was only a single field. All of this was required to accommodate the limitations of early electronic systems. The NTSC image is the crudest and most erratic of all three of the common standards and is especially poor at dealing with color. As a result, some of us translate NTSC as standing for "never twice the same color."

PAL (phase alternating line) is the broadcast standard for most other countries in the world. It came from England almost ten years after NTSC was developed. Because the English use a 50-cycle power system, PAL broadcasts at the odd rate of 25 fps. This is much closer to the 24 fps of film, and so we sometimes think of PAL as standing for "perfect at last." PAL has a higher resolution than NTSC at 625 lines per frame, though it is also divided into two fields that are interlaced. Because of its higher resolution, PAL video is sometimes used by independent filmmakers to allow a better transfer to film stock.

SECAM (sequential color with memory) is the broadcast standard for France, Eastern Europe, Russia, and Cuba. It contains 625 lines and, like PAL, runs at 25 fps. Because of its odd frame rate, SECAM equipment is virtually nonexistent in other countries. The acronym is often remembered as "system essentially contrary to American methods."

HDTV (High-Definition Television), which is being touted as the broadcast television standard of the future, represents to some the Holy Grail of the entertainment industry. It has been a long time coming; for years, those "vidiots" have been predicting that electronic media would supplant film as the format of choice for shooting everything from theatrical features to TV dramas. In the beginning, it sounded like other fantastic claims and dreams for a new technology, but now the technology is here, although a set of universal HD standards is still evolving. Theatrical features are being shot in HDTV, which produces resolution great enough to permit a successful transfer to 35mm film for theatrical distribution. Increasing numbers of episodic television dramas and variety shows, which never need to exist on film stock, and even some television movies that are not intended for theatrical release are now being shot in HDTV. This is a truly revolutionary technology.

CHAPTER

5

Video Origination and Editing: 24pHD and DV Cams

Recently, HDTV has been coupled with another advance in video technology that some claim is the death knell of film stock, and that is 24-frame Progressive High-Definition Video, or **24pHDTV.** The importance of the 24-fps frame rate is this: Film is projected at 24 fps. If you look very carefully, you'll see a certain jitter in the image, but our brains are accustomed to it, and we don't notice it. Normal video, however, screens at 30 fps, and so material that is shot with normal video looks different, primarily because there are six more frames every second, adding detail to the shot. 24p digital video cameras, however, shoot at 24 fps to simulate this phenomenon and to eliminate the problems of transferring between video and film.

Sony and Panavision have both introduced 24p HD cameras that they claim will truly provide a "film look" and will be able to replace the film medium, provide the infinite possibilities of digital processing, and save billions of dollars in the process. So energetic is the sweep of the 24p HD revolution that it is being used where budgets do not necessarily demand it. George Lucas, who has no lack of funds, chose to shoot *Star Wars, Episode II: The Attack of the Clones,* using Sony's Cine Alta 24p High Definition cameras modified for use with Panavision lenses.

Is digital really cheaper than film? If a show can be delivered on video instead of film, shooting in video can eliminate the cost of film camera assistants, film stock, processing, negative cutting, trial prints, INs, and IPs and can save a great deal of time on the set. All this is a huge savings. Since more and more film festivals can project films in video, and since the straight-to-video market is growing on television and in rental stores, more and more independent films are being shot in video, and only later will the expense of transferring to film be incurred if necessary.

However, if the show has to be transferred to film stock for distribution, which currently costs about $70,000 for the average movie, then all or most of the savings gained by the use of video will be lost at the end of the production process. For this reason, many independent low-budget movies today are still shot on 16mm or even 35mm film. (Processes are currently in development that will lower the cost of video-to-film transfers.)

DV Cams

Low-budget independent filmmakers are not terribly interested in the 24p HD versus film debate. Both of those cameras and processes continue to cost more than the average independent film can afford. Instead, independent filmmakers are now flocking to **DV Cams** (digital video cameras) as their medium of choice. Inexpensive cameras like the Sony VX-1000, Sony PD-150, and the Canon XL-I and XL-IS produce excellent results that can, with great care, be "bumped up" to 35mm film to produce a documentary look. The big push came from *The Blair Witch Project,* which was shot on cheap handheld DV Cams. It might have looked like watching dailies to most of us, but as the $120 million domestic gross rolled in, it began to look to others like a revolution. Other features shot on DV cams have followed, such as Richard Linklater's *Tape* in 2001.

The advantages of DV over both film and HD for independent filmmaking are numerous. First, of course, is cost. Home movies, once shot in 8mm film, are now universally shot in home video (except for a small cadre of 8mm enthusiasts.) The wide appeal of home video has created a market in which even high-quality video cameras have rapidly dropped in price. A high-quality DV Cam will range from $2,500 to $12,000. They can feature interchangeable lenses, built-in image stabilization for handheld shots, and sensitive pickup tubes for low-light situations. These cameras give every budding independent filmmaker a camera that surpasses the quality of what was available only a few years ago.

Second is the matter of flexibility and agility. Most video cameras are smaller and lighter than film cameras, ideal for location shooting. Video also requires less frequent reloading, since a digital videocassette holds forty to fifty minutes of material, much more than even the largest film loads; as a result, shooting can progress more smoothly. Third, digital material is far cheaper than film stock (and there is no waste or "short ends"), and the cost of film processing and shipping is eliminated. Fourth, there is no waiting for dailies; the director and DP can immediately see the result of their shooting on the set, and if the results are good, they can immediately move on to new work, striking sets and releasing actors more rapidly, all of which creates enormous savings.

It is even possible to emulate a "film look" in video, and many facilities offer various techniques to achieve this. Basically, they induce a 24-fps jitter, add some film grain superimposed over the video image, and increases the contrast. *Voila,* looks like film! This is a true boon to independents. They can shoot on DV Cam, process the results for a film look, and go to film festivals with their creations on videotape. If and when they get a distribution deal, they can go back to the original video master and transfer to film for release.

The actual all-video production process, step-by-step, is described in Figure 5.1.

Offline and Online Editing

The terms **offline edit** and **online edit** are bandied about without much accuracy these days, because the nature of the process has changed quite a bit. Basically, the editing

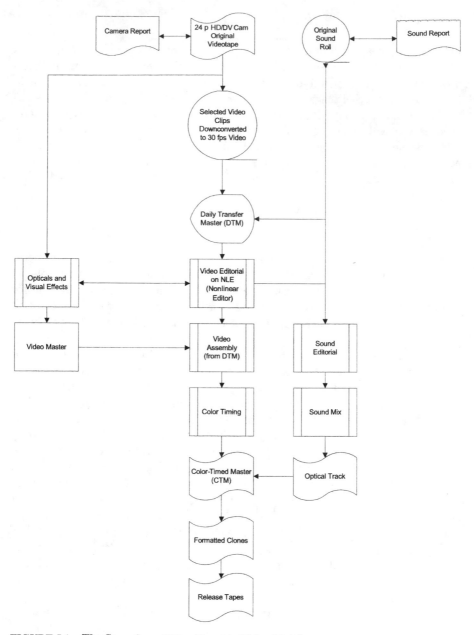

FIGURE 5.1   The Steps from Video Shoot to Video Finish.

room is *offline*. Usually, when dailies are loaded into an editing system, they are compressed to make them easier to manipulate and to save valuable storage space in the editing computer. The images that are stored in most editing computers, therefore, have about the same quality as a VHS tape, perhaps a little better. These images lack sufficient resolution to be broadcast.

Online, on the other hand, refers to any part of the finishing process that works with broadcast-quality elements. These broadcast-quality videotapes are generally either Digital Betacam, Betacam SP, D2, or high-definition tapes. Increasingly, today's powerful computer editing systems are able to store and manipulate high-resolution material without compressing it (though high-definition material must still be compressed), thus creating a finished product directly from the editing computer itself and permitting all editing to be online.

Why use offline editing at all? Why not just work at broadcast-level quality all the time? It is done partly for convenience; offline elements are quicker and easier to manipulate in the editing system. Cost is also a factor: Online systems and materials are far more expensive than offline. I would add another factor: We want to work in an atmosphere in which the creative group can collaborate with minimal financial pressure, so by using the offline-quality editing system, we can feel free to experiment. After the creative part of our editorial work is done, the broadcast-quality tapes can easily be conformed to the created show.

Conforming

Once the electronic editing is completed, the show must be prepared for delivery. The creation of this final form of the production is called **conforming.**

Nowadays, with the almost universal use of Avid, Lightworks, Final Cut Pro, or similar computer-driven editing systems, the editor simply has his or her assistant use the system to generate an **EDL** (edit decision list) in which negative key numbers are listed for each cut in the film. (At present, only the Avid system, with its patented Film Composer feature, can directly print a frame-accurate negative cut list. All the others must first convert back from 30-fps video to 24-fps film to provide frame-accurate negative cut lists.) The negative key number list is sent to the negative editor so that he or she can prepare to cut the original negative, along with Avid single-frame images for reference. For frame accuracy in cutting the negative, the negative editor uses a "lock box" that displays negative key numbers as well as time code.

Of course, if the show has been shot by using a high-resolution digital camera, such as Beta SP, there are no dailies, no telecine, and, given a high-resolution editing system, no intermediate compression. The original material, which the director and DP have viewed on the set via a carefully calibrated monitor, is loaded directly into the editing system. The saving in time, film stock, shipping, and lab costs can be enormous. (Note again that high-*resolution* video is not the same as high-*definition* video; high-definition material has to be transferred to a lower level of resolution, such as Beta SP, to be edited, so it requires additional processing steps and costs both before and after editing.)

The Future

Although film is still the medium of choice creatively, electronic media are beginning to move out of the editing room and are invading every phase of production, from Shoot to Finish. As a result, the Post process is becoming easier, faster, and more economical. For example, as we have learned more about electronic finishing over the last few years, we have been able to reduce the finishing time for a film by as much as 40 percent. This has been made possible by the significant advances in technology over the past ten years, and the most exciting thing is that this is only the beginning of the technological revolution. So much more seems just around the corner. It is hoped that with each new advance in technology, we will have the wisdom to use it to enhance the creative process, for whether we are working in film, video, or a combination of the two, the job of Post is still first and foremost to serve the story and fulfill the director's vision. Technology continues to enhance our ability to be fast and cheap; let's also remember to be good. Fortunately, we've done pretty well so far.

CHAPTER

6   The Post Schedule

I mentioned in Chapter 1 that I do not believe in an open-ended Post schedule, free of deadlines. Perhaps it is because my background has been more in television, where things move more quickly than in features, but I find that when we lose the energy provided by deadlines, we also lose some of our sense of priorities. When that happens, there can be more waste and inefficiency, and the project loses momentum and a sense of economy. As Aristotle pointed out two thousand years ago, economy is one of the qualities of beauty.

It is the function of the schedule, then, to energize the process and to establish priorities. It identifies the most important work and ensures that it is done with the proper flow of intermediate steps toward the final goal.

The Art of Scheduling

In the film business, scheduling is a fine art. Every item in a production schedule is related to every other item; a change in one resonates through the others. "Building a house of cards" is a good analogy, though I also think of postproduction supervisors as resembling jugglers adding more and more balls to those already in the air.

Schedules are laid out as far in advance as possible. If I know that a television series is going to have twenty-two episodes, I will make a calendar containing all the milestone events (dailies transfers, picture lock, sound mix, music recording sessions, delivery dates, air schedules) for every one of those episodes, taking into account weeks off, holidays, preemptions, and so on. It becomes quickly obvious if there is a problem. Perhaps the work will pile up impossibly at some point in the schedule. This leads to negotiations with the network to make sure that preemptions and repeat episodes are placed so as to solve the problem.

In features and television movies, although there is more time, the problems can be no less severe, since there are many more deadlines that must be considered. For example, press and **preview** tapes, press junkets, advertising campaigns, and distribution timetables must be addressed, the earlier the better. Frequently, we forget about all this ancillary work that is necessary for the success of a film, such as the clips about the making of the movie, the B roll and backstage interviews for the EPK, and the promotional **clips** for the stars to play on talk shows. Elements must be pulled, internegatives made, and separate mixes scheduled.

The schedule makes us all aware of the entire overview of the project, and it evolves over time. I try to review the schedule every week in a status meeting. If changes result from the meeting, I publish a new schedule, placing an asterisk at each entry that has changed, just as is done for script changes. We also publish the revised calendars using the same sequence of colors as is used for script revisions.

The Post Calendar

On the broadest level, the schedule contains the major milestones of the Post process. For a movie, these might be the deadlines for the various cuts (editor's, director's, producer's, and locked); the **spotting** session; the completion of ADR and sound preparation; the completion of opticals, titles, and visual effects; the recording of the score; the final mix; the completion of negative cutting or electronic mastering; timing; the answer print; and delivery. All these are listed on the calendar.

The main question about the calendar is, how detailed should it be? It can easily show the major steps in the process, but these major events must be preceded and followed by a host of smaller, related events. The ADR sessions, for example, must be preceded by the sound supervisor's assembly and review of the production dialogue tracks, a review of the script as per the final cut for any needed changes in dialogue, the publication of the ADR list, and the notification of cast. If the calendar tries to chart every detailed step in every process, it becomes hopelessly complex and illegible.

It is obvious, then, that one version of the calendar cannot meet the needs of everyone. The producers need only the major milestones and not the details, but at the other end of the spectrum, the editors and coordinators need an immense amount of detail, much of it specific only to them. It has taken us years to evolve a method of addressing the needs of both. (See Figure 6.1.)

The most common calendar program used in Hollywood is called *Calendar Creator.* It makes a nice, clean, legible calendar. Its main shortcoming, however, is that it is not very good at listing details, and it is not very useful for producing different versions for different uses. In recent years, we have instituted collaborative calendar sharing through a computer program called *Microsoft Outlook* instead. Although its graphics are not as familiar and as comfortable as those of *Calendar Creator,* it gives us the opportunity to quickly produce different versions of the calendar containing different levels of detail, each individualized for different users, allowing each to see the Post schedule from his or her unique perspective.

More important, *Outlook* allows us to make changes in the schedule quickly and easily and—best of all—to communicate these changes automatically to everyone who is most affected by them. Suppose, for example, that we want to make a change in the dates of the final mix. First, the scheduler of the mixing facility must make sure the stage and the mixers are available. Obviously, the producers, the director, the pic-

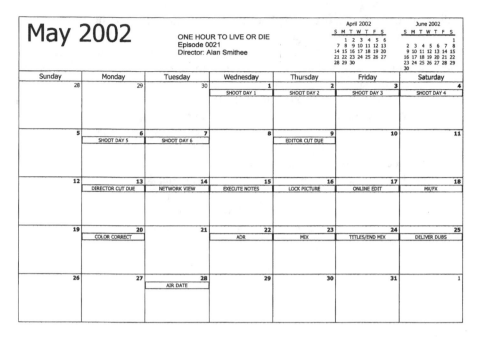

FIGURE 6.1   A Typical Post Calendar for a One-Hour Television Show.

ture editor, and the postproduction supervisor must be informed. The sound supervisor has to make sure that his or her dialogue and effects editors adjust their schedules to have the needed elements ready on the new dates. The composer and his or her music editor will have to make sure the music is recorded, prepared, and delivered to the stage on time. Perhaps the change in the final mix means that the scoring session will have to be moved; this generates a tidal wave of further changes in the schedules of the orchestrator, the copyist, the recording studio, engineer, musicians, instrument rentals, and so on. Clearly, a change of this magnitude could mean a lot of phone calls, faxes, e-mails, and chasing people down the hall.

With *Outlook,* there is a simple solution. When the initial record of each major event is created, all the people who may be affected by that event are listed on a related record called a *second page.* When a change is made in the event, the program automatically generates an e-mail to everyone on the second page with news of the change. If everyone on the team is also using *Outlook* (and we try to make it so), this e-mail contains a convenient record that they can insert directly into their calendars. There is yet a further level of interactivity available: Some of the people who receive the e-mail must approve the change, and others need to acknowledge that they have been informed. *Outlook* lets these people click on an approval button, which automatically sends a confirming message back to me.

As if this were not enough (this is beginning to sound like a Microsoft commercial), *Outlook* offers yet another critical feature. In different kinds of shows and at different times within one show, I need different kinds of scheduling information. On a series, I might need to see the airdates in relation to the mix schedule and the on-line finishing dates. On a movie, I might want to make sure the visual effects deadlines are properly timed with the integration appointments. *Outlook* provides this versatility by introducing the concept of *categories* to the scheduling process. Before I create the calendar, I create categories such as episode numbers, sound, music, editorial, and visual effects. When an event is listed in the calendar, I check off the categories related to that event. Now, whenever I need to look at a particular function, such as editorial, I can simply select that category and get the appropriate view.

The mechanics of using this system need to be learned, and it requires considerable inputting of data. The idea, however, is to do all that detail work when you have time so that you can retrieve it quickly when you don't. In the four years I've been using this system, everyone who has tried it has found it the best way to make schedule information available to everyone in the most useful form.

7 Special Visual Effects

Special effects are costly and time-consuming. They require meticulous planning during Prep, when they are designed and storyboarded so that the Shoot can take them into account, leading into each effect and coming from it so as to create a flowing, seamless sense of reality. As a picture using effects is being shot, it is not uncommon for the effects designers to visit the set and even to provide early drafts of each effect for the director and DP to use when establishing the composition and flow of the related shots. When actors are shot against a green screen in order to be placed against CGI backgrounds, for instance, they must be blocked so as to be in perfect position against the eventual created background.

When a picture is dominated by special effects, we are dazzled by the artistic conception of the effects themselves, and they become an active story element that gives us enjoyment on a level equal with that of the other dramatic elements. In truth, because so much attention and so many resources are poured into the effects, many pictures that are dominated by effects are weak on story and character, as in *Armageddon* and *Pearl Harbor,* and it is rare that extensive effects are at the service of a rich story with complex characters, as in *The Lord of the Rings: Fellowship of the Ring.*

Special effects have different uses in different kinds of film. When we think of special effects, we usually think of films set in fantasy worlds, like *Star Wars* or *Jurassic Park.* In a fantasy world, anything is possible, and the effects designers have free rein. We are eager to accept whatever they give us; it is called "the willing suspension of disbelief."

There are often more subtle but extensive special effects in highly realistic films as well, and these can sometimes be even more demanding than fantasy effects. When we are in our own everyday world, we know exactly how things should look, and we are likely to be more conscious of special effects and less willing to suspend our disbelief unless they are so superbly rendered as to be completely convincing. If they are well done, these effects become *transparent,* that is, they do not call attention to themselves but rather draw us into the story being told. Harrison Ford's escape from the bus in 1993's *The Fugitive,* for example, was a remarkable tour de force of visual effects. The scene was memorable, but the effects went largely unnoticed; they were not even nominated in the visual effects category of the Oscars that year (that Oscar deservedly went to Denis Muren for *Jurassic Park*).

There are a number of different types of special visual effects. Perhaps the simplest and oldest involve what are called **practical effects.**

Practical Effects

When you mention special visual effects nowadays, most people think of computer-generated work. But from the beginning, filmmakers and moviegoers were fascinated with visual effects, from George Melies *A Trip to the Moon* in 1902 to the original *King Kong* in 1933. These early "effects" pictures depended entirely on practical effects, that is, effects that involved creating an objective reality and then photographing it convincingly. Such effects are done, we say, *in the camera.* Melies's film featured a papier-mâché rocket ship pushed up a ramp toward the camera; the stop-motion model of *King Kong* was an early example of the kind of painstaking animation that was perfected in the Wallace and Grommet films, although the model work in *King Kong* was combined with optical or projection printing, which involves photographing from one piece of film to another, a technique that was pioneered by Linwood Dunn, A.S.C., at the RKO Studio for *King Kong* and *Citizen Kane.*

Even as late as the 1980s, many films continued to rely on practical effects. Steven Spielberg's *Jaws* in 1975 depended almost entirely on a mechanical shark, which was infamous for its unreliability. *Christine,* a 1984 film by John Carpenter, featured a classic car that killed people and, when attacked, had the power to repair itself. The various effects involved in animating the car would today be done by digital means, but Carpenter and DP Don Morgan chose to do them all "in the camera." Various mechanisms were employed in conjunction with ingenious uses of the camera, such as running the film backwards. (This was first done by Charlie Chaplin to create a convincing shot in which his toe is hit by a sledgehammer.) Even today, most pictures that involve extensive computer-generated visual effects will also use at least some practical sequences. Spielberg's *Jurassic Park,* for example, made excellent use of mechanized models for close encounters between the actors and the dinosaurs.

Perhaps the most common, and simplest, version of a practical visual effect is the so-called *poor man's process.* As an example, consider a scene between two actors driving in a car in the rain. A car is brought onto the soundstage and placed in a shallow pan made of plastic sheeting. It is surrounded on three sides by black curtains (called shooting in *limbo*), and the camera looks through the windshield as the wipers move back and forth. A rack of sprinkler nozzles spray water, fans blow the water onto the car, and grips shake the car and sweep beams of lights across it at random intervals. Perhaps small, out-of-focus points of light can be seen moving through the rear window. This simple setup can create a wonderfully believable effect.

Slightly more sophisticated than poor man's process is **process** itself. If, instead of the black curtains, our car is placed in front of a rear projection (**RP**) screen on which we project a **plate** (a segment of film) shot from the back of a moving car, we now have process. The use of rear-screen projection was perfected in the 1930s by Farciot Edouart, A.S.C., and by Charles Staffel of Pinewood Studios. It became so popular in the "golden era" of film that the studios built long, narrow soundstages called **process stages** to accommodate the throw of the rear projector.

Since all these practical effects are created in the camera during filming, they do not much concern us in Post, except insofar as they often require ADR to replace the dialogue that is ruined by water and fan noises or the wheezing and clunking of machines.

Enter the Computer

When, in the 1980s, computers became powerful enough to hold and quickly retrieve sufficient data to store and manipulate images, they began to revolutionize special effects. The era of CGI, computer-generated imagery, had dawned. The effect was felt first in television, since the relatively low levels of resolution required for TV didn't demand much computing power and even the crude early computers were up to the task. As computer power rapidly advanced, however, we soon gained the capability to economically create, manipulate, and store images with the higher levels of resolution required by feature films.

Some computerized effects are quite simple. For example, if we have a shot of the Veterans' Hospital and we have to change the name on the sign over the door to "County General," it is easy to digitize the shot and replace the old sign with a new one. This is easier, by the way, if the shot is steady, or *locked off*. If the shot needs to move, perhaps slowly push in for dramatic effect, the sign must be tracked, frame by frame. This can be done, of course, but it is a little more expensive and time-consuming.

At the other extreme, computerized effects can be extremely complex. One of my favorite films is *The Mask* (1994) with Jim Carrey. Besides CGI, it featured a variety of other effects created by live stunts, practical effects such as pyrotechnics, and large-scale models and puppets. Thirty-four percent of the total budget was devoted to these visual effects, but of that amount, only 1 percent was spent on stunts and practical effects; the rest was gobbled up by the computer. The premiere CGI production house, Industrial Light and Magic (ILM), assigned forty-five full-time employees to the film. Another fifty people worked part-time, for a grand total of 54,000 man-hours. Why was so much time needed? In the sequence in which Jim first gets the mask, for example, a sequence that lasts less than 90 seconds, more than 2,000 frames were digitally enhanced; the sequence took more than three months to complete.

Mattes and Green Screen: Cut a Hole, Fill a Hole

One of the earliest visual effects involved the use of mattes, highly detailed paintings done on glass; a scene would be photographed through the glass, and the camera was positioned so that the painted portion merged with the real scene. One portion of the frame was, in effect, cut out and replaced by the special material. This effect could also be done in Post by blacking out a portion of the frame during printing and then reprinting the blacked-out area with the special content. Even moving shots could be treated in this way through the use of a *traveling matte*. This is still the basic technique whereby any object can be matted into a shot; it is how the lettering of the credits and titles are superimposed into a movie. In all these cases, what we are doing is "cutting a hole" in the frame in some way and then filling the hole with something new.

Video technology has made this much simpler and instantaneous (it's how all those graphics and advertisements get plastered all over your favorite sporting event.) You can see it every night on the weather portion of the news when the meteorologist stands in front of the weather map and explains what's happening. He or she is actually standing in front of a colored screen, originally blue, nowadays usually green. A computer program reads the green area of the frame as a "hole" and fills it with the map, which is coming from another source. The technique is called **Chroma Key** (think of putting your key into a keyhole.) This is the famous green screen technique that can be used to let us see clouds going by outside an airplane window, a spaceship in the view screen of the Starship Enterprise, or combatants leaping from building to building in *The Matrix*. The chroma screen must be lit as evenly as possible, without shadows, and the foreground must be far enough away from the screen to avoid any reflected light from it. You must also ensure that the key color does not appear in the costumes or set, as in the story of the Hawaiian shirt in Chapter 1. See Figure 7.1 to see how a composite video effect using green screen is built.

It is even possible for the camera to move during a green screen shot by exactly recreating its movement in the motion-control camera or CGI program that provides the new background. Computer-controlled motion-control cameras have become a staple of special effects.

A new technique in which action freezes while the camera appears to sweep around the frozen figures was featured in movies like *The Matrix* and a series of Gap commercials. This effect is achieved by mounting a number of still cameras, as many as two hundred or more, about six inches apart, in a ring around the action. At the chosen moment of action, a computer triggers each camera in sequence, producing the sweeping effect. In *The Matrix,* this technique was used within a total green screen environment with actors flying from wires to produce truly astounding effects.

Morphing

In the virtual digital world of CGI, anything is possible. One of the most popular techniques, widely noticed in the *Terminator* movies, is **morphing.** This is actually a variation on a computer animation technique involving *in-betweens*. Remember, for example, the scene from *Terminator* in which the bad terminator has just been blown apart by a shotgun blast and the upper third of his body is split open, revealing its shiny metallic interior. This famous shot actually began not with CGI but with an old-fashioned practical effect: an elaborate prosthetic suit with the split-apart torso and head was worn by an actor who staggered back from the shotgun blast. This shot be-

(a)   (b)

FIGURE 7.1   A Composite Video Effect. Photo (a) shows an airfield with a wireframe outline of a Korean War Sabre Jet (taken from stock footage) moving along the tarmac. Another Sabre Jet, also taken from stock footage, has been inserted flying past from behind the hill.

Photo (b) shows the same frame as rendered. The wireframe has been covered by a "skin" of images called bitmaps taken from photographs of real Sabre jet details, and then enhanced. Note that the plane in the air has been blurred for motion and that the plane on the tarmac now has a shadow. This technique of creating wireframes of objects, animating them, then rendering them with bitmaps is now a common technique for animation and special effects.

came the starting point for the morphing sequence. A second shot was then made of the actor playing the bad terminator (Robert Patrick) undamaged, in the same position but without the prosthetic. This second shot is the destination of the morphing sequence. These two shots are laid into the computer, and it is used to make in-betweens, frames that make a smooth visual transition from the starting point to the destination. (This is also how some low-level animation is done; the animator provides only about one key frame out of six, and the computer provides the in-betweens.)

Motion Capture

It was news when George Lucas decided to create the entirely digital character of Jar Jar Binks in *Star Wars, Episode I: The Phantom Menace.* This virtual character interacted seamlessly with the live actors, with full expressive movement. This character was, in effect, an electronic full-body puppet created through the technique of **motion capture.**

A real actor, a movement specialist, was the source of Binks. The movement actor wore a black body suit that had Ping-Pong balls attached at key points, such as joints and extremities. Against a black background, the movement actor performed

Binks's actions. The Ping-Pong balls were tracked by a ring of special cameras that fired laser beams that bounced a signal back into the camera; this information was fed into a computer program that could recreate the location of each ball at every moment in a virtual three-dimensional field. These moving points were then connected so as to create a **wireframe** armature of the moving character. Just as a sculptor applies clay to a wire armature to flesh out a figure, so the computer was used to then solidify the character. This phase of the work was guided by measurements taken from detailed models of the finished character, again scanned in three dimensions by laser technology. After smoothing and various other finishing processes were applied, the image was ready to be composited into the production footage, which had been carefully shot to accommodate it. Finally, the voice was supplied in ADR by a voice actor.

Planning for Effects

As you see, many elements may be involved in a special effects shot: the principal actors, practical effects, computer objects, models, and puppets as well as green screen, matte paintings, and CGI background elements. There may be wire work (flying) or other stunts or computer characters created by motion-capture. All must work together seamlessly. If the camera is going to move, the exact nature of the move must be determined and recreated in each pass as the various elements are photographed, using computerized motion-control cameras.

Obviously, all this requires very careful planning and coordination. This is done by an effects producer or supervisor, who is either on the staff of the show or comes from the effects facility (such as ILM) that has contracted for the project. This specialist breaks down each shot in the film that requires special effects work and creates a detailed plan of how to do each shot, including both the initial shoot and Post work. All this results in a detailed storyboard that guides the creation of each shot.

8 Sound

The creative aspects of sound have been, until recently, a largely unheralded element of Post. Today's sophisticated theater sound systems, however, with multiple channels able to provide movement of sound within the theater space, huge amplifiers and specialized speakers sometimes played at nearly intolerable levels, and subwoofers that can literally shake the theater like an earthquake, have expanded the sound palette exponentially. Sound design is now a central element in the creation of a convincing and compelling world in theatrical films and even in high-quality television movies. A good sound designer goes to great lengths to create effects for a film, including recording actual on-site location sounds for the scenes as they are being filmed, collecting and manipulating prerecorded sounds, and creating entirely original sounds through various electronic processes.

All this must be done with careful attention to the needs of the story, since sound is as important as picture in setting up an audience's sense of time and place. For instance, the films *Pearl Harbor* and *In the Bedroom,* one a period action picture and the other a contemporary intimate drama, are excellent examples of differing sound requirements. In *Pearl Harbor,* the effects and backgrounds gave the audience the authentically recreated sounds of Hawaii in 1941, including period automobiles, battle scenes with sixty-year old planes, ships, explosions, and gunfire. *In the Bedroom* was a much smaller, quieter arena, but the contribution of sound was no less important. The sounds of a small town, with light traffic and atmospheric backgrounds, were designed especially to fit the locale but were also placed to provide mood and emphasis that enhanced the story. In fact, the film carefully used the absence of sound in many scenes for dramatic effect, reminding us that silence is an important element in any sound design.

The creation of a sense of reality through sound design is especially important in fantasy films such as *The Lord of the Rings: The Fellowship of the Ring.* In such films, the designer has to create sounds to fit images that have never been seen before, taking the audience into a whole new world, creating new audio sensations for a visionary film. Even in fantasy, a kind of real-world logic may operate. The sounds of the dinosaurs in the *Jurassic Park* series, for example, were mixed from a number of real animal sounds and then treated in ways that gave them qualities appropriate to the physiology of the animal. The results were not only dramatic, but also anthropologically probable.

All this takes time. Any film that involves anything other than ordinary settings would benefit from having a sound designer at work on or before the start of production, giving the director the advantage of previewing sound effects before the film has finished shooting so that he or she can incorporate them into the fabric of the film. This, of course, is partly a function of the nature of the project and the size of the budget. Low-budget independent films, documentaries, television dramas and television movies, and even smaller feature films will not usually involve a sound designer or sound supervisor until the film has been locked, if then. An $80 million action/visual effects film, however, will have a commensurately large sound effects budget, with teams of mixers working at fever pitch. *Armageddon,* for example, utilized three teams of sound editors and mixers living in trailers outside the dubbing stage, working around the clock for weeks.

The heightened use of movie sound has, in fact, altered our everyday sense of sound reality. For example, I was at a sound facility preparing for a spotting session when the infamous shootout between the Los Angeles Police Department and a group of bank robbers armed with AK47s and Uzis erupted just down the street. As we watched the live action on TV in horror, the sound designer said quietly, "Bad gunshots. They should be much bigger." Although the news helicopters were hovering directly overhead, their distant microphones picked up only tinny popping sounds from the robbers' massive firepower. A few months later, we saw some of this same footage on one of those "scariest police moments" reality shows; sure enough, the gunshots had been rerecorded and electronically enhanced and now seemed "real."

The Sound Supervisor

The sound supervisor is usually an employee of whatever sound facilities are being used for the project. Although this person is technically on the payroll of the sound studio, he or she really functions as an employee of the production and generally works exclusively on the show, with full interaction with the director, the editor, and the postproduction supervisor.

It is the function of the sound supervisor to oversee all the audible aspects of the production with the sole exception of the composed music. This includes noting the cues established at the spotting session, preparing the dialogue, supervising the recording of any additional narration, voice-overs, Walla, and ADR. The sound supervisor is also responsible for the preparatory work by the unseen, unsung sound editors who prepare the sound materials to be used in the mix. Sound design and sound effects tracks can be tricky, and the sound supervisor carefully decides how many tracks will be needed, makes sure they are filled properly with all the important sound effects, and ensures that sound design and Foley elements are being created on time. The sound supervisor attends the final mix and oversees the work of the mixers, who also "come with" the sound facility. The supervisor also works with the music supervisor or music editor to make sure all the music delivered to the mixing stage is ready on time and in the right format.

The Sound Design Process

The objective of the entire process by which the various elements that will eventually make up the sound track of a show is the final mix, or dub, when all the elements will be blended and married to the picture. There are many steps in the process, and in each step, multiple elements are prepared and gradually combined into fewer and fewer composite elements, each of which will eventually be used in the final mix. This process is graphically represented in Figure 8.1.

Perhaps no event is more important to the sound process than the original spotting sessions; separate sessions are often held for music and sound effects. At these meetings, a tape of the show containing key codes is started and stopped as the director spots the exact location of each music and sound cue and discusses the nature and function of each.

The sound supervisor numbers each cue and notes the time code for its "in" and its "out" and the content desired. If sound effects are extensive, a sound editor may also attend. A great deal of preparatory work is going to be done before the mix, and it has to be just right; once the mix starts precious time would be lost if it was necessary to procure any missing sound elements or to replace ones that did not match the director's intention.

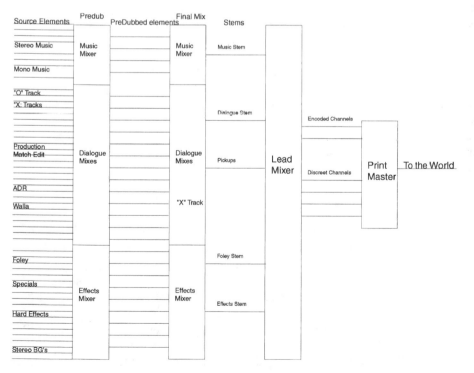

FIGURE 8.1   The Steps in Rerecording.

Once the spotting notes have been distributed to all involved, the individual editors begin work. Nowadays, sound effects editors are often called sound *designers*—and with good reason. The sound effects editors not only deal with the normal scene effects such as thunder and car sounds, referred to as the *hard* effects, but also create the many unusual and exotic sounds of the Starship Enterprise, the sound of R2D2, the Jurassic Park dinosaurs, or the almost musical automobile engine noises in *The Fast and the Furious.*

The complexity of sound effects is limited only by the imagination of the designer and the director and the number of channels of sound available on the mixing stage. As sound sources on mixing stages have been digitized, it has become more and more common to have hundreds of channels on the stage, each prelaid with various examples of a certain kind of sound (a thunder track, a gunshot track, a chicken track, and so on). These tracks are used to create layered sound effects and complex sound environments. This **layering** is the hallmark of modern sound design and often goes into even the simplest sounds.

The easiest way to understand the potential complexity of even a simple sound effect is to think of the sound of shutting a door. First, the sound editor must consider the dramatic context and function of the door sound within the story; it can't be just a generic door. There is the classic slamming of the door in anger; there is the slow, suspenseful opening of the door when the killer is creeping up on his victim (this usually includes the squeak of the hinge); there is the "whoosh" of air pushing through the door into the casino vault in *Ocean's Eleven.* All these possibilities may be indicated in the script only as "the door swings open."

Once we know what kind of door opening is needed, we begin to build the sound itself. This can involve many different sound components, many different prelaid tracks. The turning of the handle, the click of the latch, the sound of the hinge, the sound of air moving through the crack, the scraping of the door on the carpet—the sound editor will place each of these components on a separate channel and allow the sound effects mixer to create the balance during the final mix. Is it any wonder that hundreds of sound channels and sources are needed?

Foley

Foley (named for the man who invented the process) is the art (and it definitely is an art) of recording sounds produced by the action of the characters that must be directly synchronized with the picture, such as footsteps.

Foley is used to create sounds that could not be adequately controlled while on location. For instance, in a simple scene at a breakfast table, we would see actors talking as they eat with silverware, plates, and cups, all of which produce sounds that could have been distracting and overwhelming on the original production recording, and might have restricted the choices of the editor. Instead, these sounds are minimized on the set by padding the utensils or are stripped out by the editor; they are then recreated by a team of Foley artists once the cut has been locked.

This is done on a Foley stage, a place that looks like your grandmother's attic (if you have a really messy grandmother). There are piles of junk that can be used to simulate almost anything; the floor is broken up into small sections of different surfaces—asphalt, linoleum, marble, wood, stones, dirt—that are used to replace the footsteps of the actors in the film. Foley artists even come to work with several different kinds of shoes: tennis sneakers, dress shoes, high heels, hiking boots. When combined with the different floor surfaces, any kind of walking sound can be achieved. If the actors fight, the Foley artists will mimic the fight; kissing scenes probably need to have the smacking of lips enhanced. The Foley artists can make the flimsy plywood doors of the set sound like massive bank vaults, and the famous pulled punches of the actors that actually miss by several inches end up sounding like vicious body blows. All this is done quickly by one or two people using very low-tech equipment, making Foley the most economical creative element of the entire filmmaking process.

Once the Foley team has created the necessary sounds, a Foley editor cuts them to **match** the action on the picture.

You might be wondering why we go to such lengths to recreate sounds that could have been recorded during the shoot itself. True, in low-budget situations, sounds that are captured on the production track are often used to minimize the need for postproduction sound effects and Foley. Even in larger-budget projects, some sounds from the production track may find their way into the final product. However, there are several reasons why using on-set sound is problematic.

First, most sounds are difficult to capture and control on the set, where the sound recordist is rightly concentrating on the dialogue and the microphones are arranged accordingly. Second, sounds that are married to the dialogue track cannot be separately controlled to achieve the proper final mix. Finally, distribution requirements for many shows require the creation of an **M&E** (Music and Effects) version. When a show is sold to a non-English-speaking country, the English dialogue is removed, and with it all the background sounds that may have been present on the original production track. Using a clean M&E, foreign translators are able to record dialogue in the language of their country and then simply mix it with the provided sound effects and music.

Note: Four important sound elements will be covered later in this book. ADR (Automatic Dialogue Replacement), voice-over narration, and Walla (ambient human sounds) involve the work of actors and are often supervised by the editor and sometimes the director. These will both be discussed in the section on editing, Chapter 14. Likewise, the music for the show, called the underscore, is supervised by the composer and prepared for the final mix by the music editor; it will be discussed in Part Three.

Prelays and the Final Mix

As we have said, the sound editors create a myriad of tracks for possible use in any given moment in the film. It would be difficult to sort through all of these tracks and retrieve the desired sound during the final mix; as huge as most professional mixing boards are, there is a limit to the number of tracks the mixers can effectively control.

For these reasons, **sound mixers** often perform a *premix,* also called a **prelay,** for elements such as sound effects and Foley. These prelays are meant to consolidate the many tracks of the various sound elements into a more manageable number of channels, thereby saving time and confusion in the final mix. The premixes are usually supervised by the sound supervisor.

Dialogue can be especially time-consuming at the final mix, when the levels and quality of the various takes must be blended to produce a seamless flow with the proper shifts in perspective as camera angles change. A **dialogue predub** is therefore sometimes done. This is so important that it may be supervised by the director as well as by the editor and the sound supervisor.

Once all the prelays are done and the underscore has been recorded and prepared, all is ready for the final mix, technically called the rerecording or **dubbing session.** Here, all of the many dialogue, sound, and music tracks are rerecorded, or *mixed down,* into three separate channels, often referred to as stems, one each for dialogue, sound effects, and music. Each stem contains several elements. The dialogue stem may contain production dialogue, ADR, Walla, and narration. The effects stem may contain Foley and production effects. Music stems may include the original score and licensed source music for jukeboxes, radios, and so on. During the dub, each of these stems is controlled by one of the mixers.

The stems are kept separate, even after the final mix, because there are many different forms that the sound of the film may have to take for different delivery situations. Most obvious is the need for international distribution, for which the dialogue must be dubbed into foreign languages. For this, only the music and effects stems are used, creating the M&E (Music and Effects). There are also a myriad of promos, trailers, web site clips, and so on that must be provided after the film is finished. For these, the promo editors need the film without the original music so that they can compile bits of the film into a promo and then re-edit music to fit the result. This version of the picture is called the **D&E** (Dialogue and Effects).

It is imperative that the dub occur in an acoustical environment similar to the final presentation space. This means that feature films must be mixed in large mix theaters, complete with seats; for the same reason, TV mixing stages are usually fairly small and equipped with a set of small speakers that can be used to check the balance of the final mix. It may be that the loss of bass and emphasis of treble sounds on small speakers will require some adjustment of the mix.

Audio Presentation Formats

The growing importance of sound as a creative element is reflected by the proliferation of audio systems and processes that are now prominently featured in the marketing of many films. Most of them replace the traditional optical sound track with technical audio encryption processes such as the Dolby Digital Sound system. Sony markets a process call *SDDS* that places the sound for the movie on a separate CD that runs in sync with the picture. All these are designed to make the sound as alive, clear, and natural as possible.

Digital sound is sometimes played at levels that can overwhelm a theater's sound system (not to mention the audience's ears). To make sure that each theater is reproducing sound correctly, LucasFilm pioneered THX, named after George Lucas's first film. This is not a sound process but rather a sound *standard.* The THX logo assures the audience that the audio equipment in that particular theater has been examined and meets the exacting standards demanded by THX. Anyone who has spent his or her hard-earned money on a highly anticipated film only to listen to a speaker crackling throughout the movie can thank the people at THX for their contribution.

9 Prints, Distribution, and Archives

The final stage of any project is the delivery of the film prints or video dubs for distribution. In today's world of international distribution, this can be a very complex affair. The requirements of the various forms of delivery need to be considered even before shooting begins, although the most important preparations for delivery happen in Post.

Film Prints

When a film is printed, the exposure settings must be adjusted, shot by shot and scene by scene, to achieve a consistent look. This process is supervised by the DP and a timer, and is described in Chapter 14.

We mentioned earlier that release prints are made from an internegative. These prints incorporate either an optical soundtrack that is *print mastered* at the conclusion of the final mix or the information needed to permit one of the newer digital sound formats to synchronize a separate audio source with the film when it is projected.

16mm film prints are almost totally obsolete. Feature films are distributed internationally as 35mm film prints broken into reels. Each reel, about 1,000 feet long and about ten minutes in running time, is coded for switchover to the next reel. (You might have noticed the little circles that appear in the upper right-hand corner of the film that signal the switchover.) Some larger theaters have projectors that can hold several reels at one time, and at these theaters the projectionist will splice reels together.

A few major feature films are shown in 70mm at the few theaters that are capable of showing this large format. At one time, these might have been shot on 65mm film and then released as 70mm prints. Nowadays, however, when so few 70mm prints are needed, they are invariably blown up from original 35mm interpositives.

Video Distribution

Theatrical distribution aside, video distribution of most movies far exceeds film distribution; international broadcasts and videocassettes have replaced film in many applications. We discussed earlier the dominant video formats: NTSC in North American and Japanese television, PAL in Britain and Europe. It is often assumed that the quality of the PAL system exceeds that of the NTSC system because each PAL frame contains 100 more lines than an NTSC frame, but the amount of information is actually the same. NTSC runs 30 frames per second at 525 lines, and this provides the eye with almost exactly the same amount of information as PAL's 25 frames per second at 625 lines. The quality of the PAL image does appear better, however, because there are more lines in each scan, resulting in higher resolution.

Just as in film, the quality of the television picture is very dependent on the quality of the originating image, but unlike film, this can be radically affected by the tape format in which the image is delivered. Videotape comes in two distinct formats: **component** and **composite.** The idea of a *component* system is to separate the electronic signal into its relative components and transmit them on separate channels. Because each channel is carrying less information, the quality of each is enhanced. Unfortunately, the extra channels for the separated signals make component systems expensive. The *composite* format, by contrast, mixes all the primary channels into a single signal before recording. The videos that you rent or buy in the store are composite recordings that are much cheaper to produce. The more expensive component format is used only in the studio for production and the creation of visual effects.

Just as film gave way to videotape, videotape is giving way to tapeless formats for distribution. **Hard disk** digital formats such as **DVD** (digital video disc) are steadily replacing VHS tapes in the video stores. The hard disk holds much more information and allows interactive program content to be mass distributed without the complications of complex playback systems.

Eventually, even the DVD may give way to systems that can store many films on hard drives. Already, hard drive formats are being used for broadcast and projection projects. Although these excursions are largely experimental, it is certain that electronic projection systems will continue to invade theaters in the next few years. This trend could eventually eliminate the hundreds of tape cassettes and DVDs that now clutter our offices and homes.

Final Delivery

Someone once said that films aren't finished, they are only abandoned. For the postproduction supervisor, however, the job is not finished until every item required by a very specific set of contractual delivery requirements has been delivered to the network, studio, or other financing entity. Obviously, this includes the film in its final form (often in more than one format). If the show was shot in film, this will include delivery of the original negative, the IN and the IP, and perhaps a low-contrast print. If it was shot in video, this will include the original video elements and video masters.

In either case, the original sound elements are also required, along with the musical scores and all cue sheets. Also required is a mountain of accumulated paperwork for the production, including everything from the Shoot that was sent to Post and the paperwork created during Post itself.

In addition to the show itself and its related original components, elements necessary for dealing with international release must also be delivered. M&E stems (music and effects with no dialogue) and textless visual elements (that is, frames that originally contain superimposed cards or titles must be supplied with the text removed). All this is necessary so that other languages may be inserted. D&E stems (dialogue and effects with no music) might also be required for the preparation of promotional materials such as trailers and promos, which will be given their own music. The original music score is often required for subsequent release of a soundtrack album. Additional elements may be demanded if the movie has unusual postproduction elements, such as blueprints for models and miniature sets or special costumes and makeup.

The best rule to follow is "Save it all." If there is even a remote possibility that something might be of use later on, put it in the archive vault. If nothing else, someone else will throw it out years later; let them take the blame for ruining history. The last and perhaps most important item, from a legal point of view, is the *proof of delivery.* I make it a point to get a signed receipt of final delivery that lists every single element that goes to the studio or network and to the vault. I then send copies of these receipts with two cover letters, one stating explicitly that the film was delivered on such and such a date to the studio or network and another listing all of the elements that I have delivered to the archive vaults. Only then is my job finished and not abandoned.

Archives

There have been many heartbreaking reports recently of important old films rotting away as the nitrate stock on which they were printed disintegrates. A few have been saved: A passionate projectionist in France kept the films he exhibited in a good vault and thus preserved them; some important master negatives have been uncovered in the homes of their makers or in even more unlikely places. Countless more have been lost. Even fairly recent major films are in danger. Already, restoration is underway on films that are less than forty years old, such as Martin Scorsese's *Mean Streets* and Stanley Kubrick's *2001: A Space Odyssey.*

One wonders why these films were not more carefully stored. You must realize, however, that the studios and the distributors are businesses, not museums; for them, film is a commodity. After it has served its purpose, the further expense of proper archival storage, which reduces the bottom line, is not a high priority. Sometimes, films are lost or destroyed through plain carelessness. For example, Walt Disney was so angry after the initial failure of *Fantasia* in 1940 that he had the film chopped into smaller pieces to be distributed by his new educational division. *Fantasia* was the very first theatrical release with stereo sound, but the educational films, projected in class-rooms, were monaural, so the two original stereo tracks were mixed into one. Even after the film was later restored to its original form, the monaural version was the only one available for many years. Not too long ago, however, the missing stereo track was discovered accidentally in a Disney vault, leading to the rerelease of the film with its orginal stereo soundtrack forty years after the original premiere.

How best to archive film? There is a myth that digital elements will last forever. Although it is true that a digital original can be copied infinitely with no degradation between generations, the digital information itself degrades after about ten years, and if no fresh copy is made, it will be lost. Digital archives, then, depend on regular re-copying, which is costly over the years. Digital is not the answer.

The very best way to archive film is to transfer it to special black-and-white archival stock. A color film is run through three filters that separate the three primary film colors: cyan, magenta, and yellow; each is rendered as a black-and-white record that can recreate the film when the process is reversed. However, if these three records were stored on separate pieces of film, there is the danger that they could stretch and go out of sync when printed; instead, the three records are printed as alternating frames on one strip of film. When a print is needed, a special printer reverses the process. Archived in this way and stored under proper conditions, a film can last over a hun-dred years.

It is not difficult to store film and videotape in a climate-controlled atmosphere, with proper temperature and humidity and a guarantee that these conditions will not change. All you need do is find a cave about fifty feet or more below the surface of the earth; there the conditions are ideal. In Lawrence, Kansas, as well as other places, there are large natural vaults, created thousands of years ago during the glacial period in North America, that are capable of storing thousands of reels of film and videotape. There are also human-made climate-controlled vaults throughout the world, with computer-controlled air conditioning and humidifiers.

Several elements should be archivally stored in addition to the final cut of the film, including the original cut negative, internegatives, and interpositives. It is also wise to store the videotapes that are used to edit the film, although debate rages about how these tapes will be played in thirty years if no one saves the machines that are used to play them. I have a show of mine on a forty-year-old reel of two-inch high-band color videotape that can't be played today.

The problem of archiving involves more than the films themselves; Hollywood has a cavalier attitude toward most of its own artifacts. In the so-called golden era of the movies, the studios kept all sorts of elements that had been used in the making of films, but as the space and cost of this storage grew and studio leadership passed from the moguls to the bureaucrats, they began to discard things. Years ago, for example, I participated in a revival of *War of the Worlds,* a series made at Paramount in the 1950s. Wanting to recreate the original spaceships, we contacted Paramount's spe-cial effects department. Unfortunately, they had auctioned off not only the spaceship models that had been in their vaults for years, but also the plans that had been used to create the originals. Fortunately, a Hollywood modelmaker, Greg Jean, had bought them and was able to recreate the originals exactly as George Pal had filmed them years ago.

This sort of luck is just that—luck. We should not have to depend on luck to save our cinematic past. The truth is that until Hollywood is convinced of the importance of its own historical past, films will continue to be lost. Thankfully, dedicated film preservationists are making efforts to save what they can. Support them in any way you can.

PART TWO

Editing

MICHAEL BROWN, A.C.E.

Editing is not a *technical* process.
It is an *artistic* process.
It is about storytelling.
What editors do, is the final rewrite of the script.
—Jack Tucker, A.C.E.

10 The Editor, the Director, and the Editing Team

Editing is sometimes thought of as a merely mechanical process, a sort of paint-by-numbers, and in some situations, especially in television, it can be. But even in the most mundane situations, and certainly in any serious cinematic work, editing requires certain artistic talents. Just as an actor has to have an instinct for role-playing, so the fledgling editor must have an instinct for storytelling, timing, and rhythm. These are the essentials of the editing process.

It is extraordinary how much the editor's taste and personality can influence a film. I recently judged work by a group of ten college student editors; they had all been given the same raw footage, the same takes of the same script, and had been asked to edit it into a ten-minute film sequence. It was amazing how different the results were, not only in a technical sense, but in style, tone, and meaning as well. It was obvious which of these students had a natural affinity for the editing process and which did not.

Even a novice editor can cut film together well enough to get from the beginning to the end of a story. That much is simple. What separates the novice from the professional is their sense of *context,* the ability to shape and focus the story, to create a dramatic flow and development, to expose the thought processes of the characters, and to guide the viewer's attention to the most meaningful details. This is achieved by making literally thousands of subtle choices, moment by moment, without ever losing the perspective of how each individual choice fits into an unbroken chain of images that are ultimately experienced as a single, meaningful event.

This requires not only the natural talent to see how every individual moment of the film fits into the overall story, but also the tremendous stamina that is required to sustain this effort day after day for weeks and even months. Many people who set out to become editors fall by the wayside after spending just a few weeks in the editing room as take after take of the same bit of business, the same exchange of dialogue, is run over and over again, different combinations of takes and angles are tested, and subtle changes are made in the placement and duration of a cut. Unless one is completely involved in the story and can sustain this focus over time, the work can quickly become tedious.

A sense of storytelling, context, rhythm, and timing, along with stamina, then, are the key skills of the editor. We must add to this list skills of collaboration, especially the ability to work well with a director.

The Relationship between Editor and Director

Except in some television situations, editors seldom work alone, and the various relationships between the editor and his or her fellow workers are important to the development of an editing career and to the work itself. The most important and special of these relationships, of course, is that between editor and director.

Several factors endanger the relationship of editor and director. First, they are profoundly dependent on one another for the success of their work. Second, the boundaries between their creative territories overlap, creating a situation that can inflame egos if both are not secure in their own creative identities. Third, their relationship is subject to the special pressures of deadlines, budget, and the demands of the producers. Finally, during shooting, the director and editor often work at some distance from one another. Few relationships in life are as sorely tested.

But when these pitfalls are avoided and a real meeting of the minds is achieved, the working relationship of an editor and director can be a wonderfully exciting creative pairing that can inspire each of them to achieve results they would be incapable of alone, a pairing that is truly greater than the sum of its parts.

Ideally, an editor will be so in tune with a director's vision of the film they are making that their ideas will flow as one, in perfect alignment. Though rare, this is the ideal toward which editors and directors strive, and when it is achieved, a long-term creative relationship usually results.

Forming the Relationship

The first time an editor and a director work together, it feels a little like going out on a blind date. They have to spend time getting to know one another, testing the chemistry between them, learning how best to communicate, developing respect for one another's values and idiosyncrasies, and finding a basis for mutual trust. The process begins at the very first meeting between the director and a prospective editor. The best approach is for the editor to supply the director (or producer, if it's a television series) with a *reel,* a cassette with examples of his or her most recent editing efforts. This reel might contain sections of theatrical films, television movies, episodes of a television show, documentaries, or student work. Even more important than a reel are the recommendations of the two or three directors and/or producers with whom the editor has recently worked. These people will provide information regarding not only the editor's skills, but also his or her personality, conscientiousness, and relationships with the other members of the filmmaking team.

Let's assume that the "first date" has gone well and the editor has been hired. There follows a sort of "honeymoon" during which the director and editor start to establish communication and trust, often while the director is already shooting in some distant location. During this crucial period, the editor will be wise to send the director samples of edited sequences from the very first material shot in order to establish trust and to ensure that the work is moving in the right direction. The editor is guided in this early work by his or her discussions with the director about the intended tone, pace, and other qualities of the show. The director may even be using a **storyboard,** a sequence of drawings showing the composition of major shots and the transitions between them, and if so, the editor will use the storyboard as a guide. It is also useful for the editor to have watched as many of the director's previous films as possible to get a sense of the director's finished style. Ideally, these first assembled sample scenes or sequences are screened with the director in person, or they might be sent to the location on tape. The editor and the director can then discuss, in person or by phone, the choices that have been made and the reasons behind those choices.

If these early sequences meet with the director's approval, both editor and director are immediately relieved. Even if the director does not like the samples, there is time to discuss the material so that the editor can adjust his or her thinking to match the director's intent. The important thing about this approach is that the editor and the director are both working with real and specific material, thus avoiding the ambiguity of words, which can mislead them into thinking they agree when in fact they don't—or vice versa.

If the editor and director get along well and even become friends, it makes the work more pleasant and can speed the development of trust and openness. But what happens when the personalities of the editor and director clash? Though this can be unpleasant, the editing process can still work as long as there is respect for each other's talent and abilities. One of my fellow editors has had a very successful career working with a director with whom, under other circumstances, he probably couldn't relate. They bicker back and forth, challenging one another in a kind of competitive warfare. Surprisingly, their work is enriched by their differences. The important thing is that even though each one wants to score the most points, they're on the same team. They even keep a scorecard on the wall of the editing room, allocating points for the best editorial ideas. After the film is finished, the winner chooses the most expensive restaurant he can find, and the loser buys dinner! At last count, they're about even after eight films together.

Every creative person has a forceful ego, whether it is obvious or not, and people with strong egos often dislike having their choices challenged. But in a secure, creative relationship between editor and director, both allow their choices to be questioned because they trust one another and have a shared goal. In fact, differing ideas and opinions, when dealt with constructively, can be invaluable; wonderful things can result when a director and editor disagree but are willing to listen to one another. Working out disagreements often produces unexpected results that are better than what either the editor or director might have imagined on his or her own.

There is another necessary quality of a good working relationship: honesty. The editor is in a very special relationship with the director because he or she is the first person to see the results of the director's work, and to judge it with an understanding of what the director is trying to accomplish. When the director asks the editor how he or she feels about the script or the previous day's dailies, the editor must be candid and honest in sharing his or her real thoughts and not simply say what the editor thinks the director would like to hear. We editors are artists entitled to and responsible for our own judgments. Such honest feedback, thoughtfully expressed, must be given directly and privately to the director—and only to the director. It is far more valuable than mere lip service, even when it might be painful. The director, in the midst of shooting, needs an objective eye and must have confidence in the editor's informed and honest opinion.

Tact

One of the most important qualities an editor needs in dealing not only with directors but also with producers, executives, and the members of the editing team, is tact. There are a number of dangerous political quagmires into which an editor can fall that can be avoided only by the exercise of great tact.

One such situation is when a producer or executive, who may in fact have hired the editor, secretly asks to view edited scenes without first receiving the director's permission. This places the editor in a very awkward ethical position, and there is only one right course of action, one that is supported by the rules of the Directors Guild of America (**DGA**). In a firm but reasonable manner, the editor must explain to the producer that he or she is welcome to see the material once the director has given his or her okay, adding that it wouldn't be fair to run edited film behind the director's back.

Another sticky situation arises when uninvited guests try to visit the editing room and look at material in process. Generally, all work prior to the release of the director's cut must be regarded as confidential, and no one should see it until all concerned have agreed to its being made public. Even those connected with the film should be kept at bay. Actors sometimes ask if they can sneak a peek at their performances; the correct response is to tell them to get permission from the director first. They will seldom be back.

Some actors have tricks designed to generate screen time, such as "throwing away" the master shot to force the editor to use their close-up. Some may even try to ingratiate themselves to the editor in hopes of winning more screen time. When I was editing a miniseries in Paris, one such leading lady took an inordinate interest in me. She went out of her way to be friendly, even flirtatious, and I found myself the recipient of a number of warm hugs. It was obvious what she was after, and it wasn't me; she wanted more coverage in the film, especially her close-ups. I politely assured her that I would do my best to give her all the coverage her scenes required. I next saw her at the party after the premiere of the movie. She didn't even smile in my direction.

The situation that requires the greatest tact, without doubt, arises when an editor finds himself or herself caught in the middle of a war between a director and a producer. This, unfortunately, is not uncommon, since editors work at the very point at which the powerful egos and visions of producers and directors most often collide. A producer might have a difference of opinion with the director about a particular scene, and the producer, hoping to get an ally, will ask the editor for his or her opinion. Even with the greatest tact, expressing an opinion in this kind of situation can be hazardous. The answer given may be quoted, or misquoted, as proof that "the editor agrees" with one or the other. It's a dangerous game, one to be avoided if possible.

In many ways, the relationship between editor and director is like a marriage, and it is not surprising that many editors and directors enter into long-lasting partnerships that grow and become richer with each passing film. Producers must respect such established relationships whenever possible, even when money is in short supply. The editing budget is a small percentage of any film's total cost, and it doesn't pay to be penny wise and pound foolish by hiring the wrong editor, even if it saves money initially. There is rarely time for an editor to be replaced during shooting, and recutting after shooting is costly. Indeed, it is when budgets are tight and shooting schedules are rushed that the editor can be most important to the success or failure of a film. A skillful and creative editor, working in good alignment with his or her director, can be the best investment a producer can make.

To sum up, the relationship between editor and director can take many forms. Friendship can be important and makes the job more pleasant, but more important are good communication, mutual respect, honesty tempered by diplomacy, and a sense of common purpose that puts the best interests of the film above all others. Even given all these qualities, it is only in the process itself, working together day by day in the trenches, the baptism of fire in which editor and director fight the fight to make the best film possible, that we can really get to know one another and produce results that neither of us would be capable of alone. At its best, the creative relationship between editor and director can be greater than the sum of its parts.

The Editing Team

The editing room (usually a suite of rooms) is a special place. Darkened, often hushed, it reflects the nature of the work done there: reflective and intently focused, serious even when playful, and endlessly repetitious. The relationships between all the people who work in this space or may visit it can be crucial, and behavior in an editing room is governed by special considerations and customs.

The most important member of the editor's team is the assistant editor, who is the editor's right-hand man or woman. The **IATSE** (International Alliance of Theatrical Stage Employees) contract of the Editors Guild states simply that the assistant editor's job is to assist the editor in the completion of his or her assignment. That can mean a lot of things, and the better the assistant, the more it can mean. At best, this can be a long-term, symbiotic relationship, and the editor and assistant come to know one another so well that they can act as one. The relationship also has the qualities of mentor and mentee, for the assistant editor is an "editor-in-waiting" who will eventually move up through the ranks and become an editor in his or her own right.

In the meantime, the assistant editor is expected to be as quiet as a church mouse while the director and the editor are working and not blurt out opinions unless asked. As the assistant gains experience and the editor becomes convinced that he or she knows the ropes, the assistant begins to work with the editor in editing scenes. After they have worked together successfully on a few scenes, the editor might let the assistant begin to execute changes, such as dropping portions of scenes. Some editors will leave the mechanics of rendering choices on the editing system to the assistant, so that the assistant functions as the editor's hands, executing his or her thoughts about the cuts and leaving the editor free of the mechanics of the process. In such cases, the assistant might know more about the actual operation of the editing system and its frequent upgrades and problems than the editor does. The moral support, technical savvy, and ingenuity of the assistant editor, especially when problems arise, can make the difference between a disaster and a truly creative solution.

On a large project, there may be more than one assistant editor (on a huge effects movie, there may in fact be more than one editing team). Even on a modest project, there may, in addition to the assistant editor, be an apprentice editor or a production assistant assigned to the editing team. All these people must have certain qualities if the team is to function at its best.

First, a good editing team member should contribute to an overall positive feeling in the editing room. Editing is intense, sustained, even sometimes boring work, and even a little negativity can grate on everyone's nerves over the long haul. Conversely, an optimistic, steady person can be a tremendous support when the going gets rough, as it always does at some point in every film.

It is also desirable for assistants and apprentices to have a touch of humility and compassion, to avoid criticizing the work in order to win points or to show off. The rumor mill in a film company tends to be hyperactive, and if someone on the editor's crew makes stupid comments after viewing dailies, they are likely to reach sensitive ears and create friction. The denizens of the editing suite also need a good sense of humor to lighten the many tedious hours. Most important of all, they must take pride in their work and have a conscientious commitment to doing the best work possible under the circumstances.

Style

An editor's taste and personality inevitably influence the films he or she cuts. However, this is not the same as saying that an editor has a particular personal style that overrides the stylistic qualities of the script or the director's style. An editor who imposed a personal style to such a degree would be doing a disservice to the director and to the film. An editor must work in consort with the director's vision and with sensitivity to the inherent qualities of the material.

In sitcoms and episodic television drama, for example, a style for a given show is developed by the producers, the writers, and, in some cases, the original director. Shows such as *Will & Grace* or *The West Wing* have an established style that comprises a certain kind of writing, a certain manner of performance, and a specific visual style. These qualities become the signatures of the show and are instantly recognizable. All guest writers, directors, and performers must conform to this style, as must all the editors who work on the show.

In so-called **long form** (movies for television and theatrical features), the style is more individual to the specific film, although various genres carry with them cinematic traditions that establish a kind of vocabulary and grammar of editing techniques. The western, the romantic comedy, the psychological thriller, the chase movie, and the other genres all have such traditions. Even when a director chooses to depart from such conventions, the editor must have a sense of the conventions that are being broken. The style of the individual film, then, exists within the context of cinematic tradition and results from the choices made by the producers in the development of the material, the style of the writer, and eventually the director's way of translating the script to film. The director's vision also informs the work of the cinematographer (DP) in establishing the film's visual style and the work of the actors in creating their performances. All this is established before the editor begins his or her work and must be taken into account so that the editor's work flows consistently from the choices that have already been made. Even on those rare occasions when a film is shot in a very neutral way that invites aggressive editing, the film will be shaped and given a sense of style in the editing room with the active participation of the director.

In all, then, a good editor must be a skillful collaborator. This does not mean that he or she is a mere mechanic, blindly following the director's instructions. Rather, the editor must be able to align himself or herself with the director's vision in a manner that extends, enhances, and sometimes challenges that vision in a way that moves the film toward its fulfillment.

11 The Work Begins

The material that is shot each day is sent to the editing room as quickly as possible. In the old days, these were pieces of developed, printed film, called *dailies.* As you learned in Chapter 3, these film dailies were then cut by hand on a movieola or flatbed and assembled into a *workprint.* Many of the terms used in today's computer-driven editing systems come from that film era, such as *scene **bins,** trims,* and *split tracks.*

Nowadays, the dailies come not on film but on videotape or in digital form. As you learned in Part One, going from film to digital is relatively simple, even when the show has been shot on film. Once the film negative has been developed in the lab, it is transferred directly, without printing, to a master tape format. The lab or transfer house will then sync up the video picture to a copy of the original audio track that was made on the set. This combined editing copy is delivered to the editing room, inserted into an Avid or comparable editing computer, and loaded onto the computer's hard drive either directly or through a process called **digitization** at whatever level of resolution the editor has chosen (see Figure 11.1). This is the start of the digital editing process that finally ends with the delivery of an answer print, either on film or in a digital format.

The Lined Script and the Assistant Editor's Log

As the film is being shot, daily communication between the editing room and the set is critical and is facilitated by the **script supervisor.** This is the person who sits next to the director on the set and keeps a continuous record of all scenes as they are shot. These unsung heroes are responsible for **continuity,** making sure that it will be possible to cut from take to take with everything matching: the words, the actors' positions, the amount of water in a glass and on which line of dialogue the actor drank—in short, everything down to the smallest detail. This is no small feat, especially when hours and even days might elapse between one take and another in a given scene. The script supervisor also notes which takes are to be printed and the total pages shot each day and provides a timing of each scene that is compared to the original estimate and

FIGURE 11.1   An Avid Editing System. From left to right on the top level are the stereo speakers for sound, two monitors that are tied together to provide one wide workspace for the actual editing process, and the single monitor that displays the result of the editing. On desk level are various patching components that allow different sources to be routed to various destinations, a small sound mixing board, and at the far right a printer for printing EDLs and other forms. Under the desk are the power source that prevents the loss of information if power fails, the tape players (in this case a VHS and a Beta SP), the central processing unit (CPU) of the Macintosh computer that drives the system, and at far right the tower holding the various hard disk drives that store all the data.

is useful in determining whether the show is running long or short. When asked, the script supervisor might even advise the director about **eye-lines** and whether further coverage is needed for a scene.

Most important, the script supervisor records the specifics of every shot in his or her script for the guidance of the editor. The script supervisor records each shot and each printed take on his or her script (called the **lined script**) with special markings and notations. These pages are sent along with the dailies to the editor and are invaluable in guiding him or her in assembling the rough cut of each scene (see Figure 11.2). On the lined script, each take is marked by a line indicating where it starts and where it ends. The squiggly lines indicate lines spoken off camera, and the solid lines mark those spoken on camera.

Besides marking each shot on the script, the supervisor writes notes about each shot on the clean reverse side of pages that face the script text. These notes describe the shots as master shots, over-the-shoulder shots, medium shots, close-ups, or any other shot configuration the director uses. Along with this description, the script

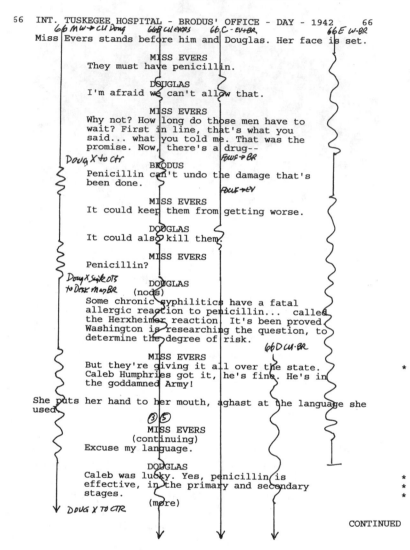

FIGURE 11.2   A Script Supervisor's Lined Script.

supervisor will offer a short explanation of the camera's movement and give timings in minutes and seconds from the start of the take to the end. If several takes have been printed, the supervisor will indicate which ones are preferred. The notes will also contain any other important information that might be of use to the editor, such as warnings of soft focus or takes with incomplete or bad sound.

The information that the script supervisor's notes supplies is sometimes augmented by daily conversations between the editor and the director. Under the pressures of shooting, things can change rapidly, and the editor must be up-to-the-minute. Scenes can be rewritten, trimmed, or completely dropped, and this often results in the need to make changes in scenes that have already been assembled. The editor will have to review his or her cut material and possibly re-edit to adjust for different transitions, changes in dialogue references, and so on.

When the video dailies arrive in the editing room, they are logged by the assistant editor using several references such as shooting day, scene, shot, and take numbers. The dailies also carry the imbedded files (the *metadata,* or flex files) described in Chapter 4. These are the **audio time code** created on the set, the video time code created when the dailies were produced, and, if film has been used, the film frame numbers. These reference numbers are displayed in **windows** on the image of the daily itself (see Figure 11.3). Although today's computerized and digital systems make the assistant editor's job far less onerous than it once was, these logs must be accurate and

FIGURE 11.3   A Daily with Windows. The audio time code is in the upper left window, the video time code is in the lower left, and the film frame numbers (the key code) is in the lower right. The actor is Joe Morton in HBO's *Miss Evers' Boys,* directed by Joseph Sargent, produced by Robert Benedetti, and edited by Michael Brown.

are invaluable for locating needed takes during editing, especially at those rare but crucial times when rejected takes that were never printed (B negative) must be retrieved to solve some problem. Later, if the video version of the edited film must be translated into actual cut film negatives, the computer-driven editing system automatically produces lists that coordinate the edited video with the frame numbers on the original negatives, but there may be times when the assistant editor's logs are called on to reconcile discrepancies.

Next, the various printed takes of each shot and the various shots in each scene are arranged in a logical way that allows the editor to retrieve them quickly. In the rare cases in which the editor is cutting directly on printed film, the strips of film are hung on racks, the heads up with the slate identifier ready to hand, and the bulk of the film is jumbled in a canvas basket below. More usually, a **nonlinear editing** or digital editing system is used. If an Avid (currently the most popular editing system) is used, scene bins are created, and within each bin are all the individual takes the editor may need to edit the scene. When the assistant editor breaks down the dailies into individual scenes, he or she places them into these bins and selects a single frame that best represents each particular take and marks it as a reference image. Other editing systems, such as Final Cut Pro and Lightworks, have similar ways of storing and marking takes and individual frames for reference. Whatever the system that is used, once the dailies have been broken down into bins and logged and arranged for the editor's use, the main body of the work begins.

What Can Go Wrong, Will

Viewing the dailies from the first days of shooting is an especially anxious time for an editor. Problems that appear now can affect the entire show if they are not corrected at once. To make matters worse, these first few pieces of film are closely scrutinized by a host of important people: producers, executive producers, coproducers, studio or network executives, completion bondsmen, financial backers and/or their lawyers, secretaries, wives, husbands, or significant others, all eager to spot any hint of future trouble, either creative or logistical, all eager to help direct and edit the film. The telephone begins to ring. Alarm bells are sounded. Comments begin to roll in as individuals voice their opinions and criticisms. These comments can indicate serious problems or inconsequential ones, but they all have to be addressed and considered.

The criticisms that are most normally heard are those regarding sound ("I couldn't understand her when she turned around"), cinematography ("It's too dark!"), cast ("He doesn't seem scary enough"), wardrobe ("I hated her sweater"), makeup and hair ("I can't have that hairdo in my film"), the art department ("We don't want them to look *that* poor"), set decorating ("Is that dinnerware really from the thirties?"), and location ("I know its Toronto, but can't you make it look a little more like Vietnam?").

When a criticism is voiced, the first step is to consider the source. Of course, honest and intelligent opinions, when voiced diplomatically and to the proper people, are always welcome. But the last thing an editor needs or wants to hear is unsolicited critical comments from individuals who are not qualified to voice them. I once had to explain to a network executive why a person on the telephone in Australia at night was speaking to someone in San Francisco in the daytime. The alternation between night in Australia and day in San Fransisco seemed to this executive a mismatch, and even a lesson in basic geography did little to put the objection to rest. Though it might be necessary to pay lip service to such people, the editor can choose to protect the director by absorbing and defusing the comment so that it never goes beyond the editing room.

Next, the editor must weigh the seriousness of the problem. Sometimes the problems are minor, simple matters of differing tastes and styles. These can be discussed with the director and corrected, if the director is amenable to the change. For example, changes in wardrobe, hair, and makeup or minor changes in an actor's performance can usually be accommodated in subsequent scenes without reshooting. Many things that seem to be creative problems are in fact merely differing perceptions or expectations among the producers, supervising executives, and the director. This is not uncommon, and these problems of perception will eventually work themselves out, with or without bloodshed. But some problems go to the very heart of the storytelling process and may manifest themselves only gradually as shooting progresses.

An editor can often see such problems evolving before anyone else does. When this happens, the editor must talk to the director as soon as possible and have the director set aside time to view the problematic material and discuss it with the editor. The director is almost always smart enough to see the problems that are emerging. It might be a flaw in the structure of the story, and omitting a scene or writing a new scene will remedy it and restore the story line. An actor might have been miscast or might simply lack the talent required to play the role, and recasting or bringing in a coach (*dialogue coach*) to do special work with the actor might be necessary. It might be a problem rooted in the director's manner of shooting, such as a lack of coverage or missing close-ups. It might be a problem of continuity, such as coverage that has a different tempo from the master, action that doesn't match, or an actor's performance that varies from master to coverage. There is no easy answer to any of these problems, and at these times, the editor's problem-solving abilities come to the fore. He or she must analyze the problem and define the available options for its solution with tact and a positive spirit. In dealing with creative individuals who are under pressure from many sources, it is always advisable to temper bad news with helpful ideas.

Early Technical Problems

There are other problems that are purely technical, and although such problems are often minor, they can cause major upsets when prejudged by inexperienced individuals who are prone to panic. In these cases, the editor must quickly separate fact from fiction, thus defusing a potentially explosive situation before it causes unnecessary tension. For example, I once received a set of dailies from a film shoot in which all the takes of one actor's close-ups were slightly out of focus (**soft focus**), a failing that was too subtle to have been noticed on the tiny monitors used for the video assist on the set. I contacted the director at once and informed him of the situation. We then worked with the DP to determine the source of the problem. Clearly, either the actor had missed his mark, the camera was malfunctioning, or the focus puller had made a mistake. In this particular case, we quickly determined that the problem was in the camera itself, and it was corrected easily. Once we were certain it wouldn't happen again, we discussed whether reshooting the close-ups was necessary. I offered several options, such as staying with the master, using the existing over-the-shoulder coverage, or blowing up one of the existing medium shots to create a close-up. In this case, we found a way to cut around the soft close-ups without reshooting. The scene was assembled and sent to the producers, who remained blissfully unaware that a problem had ever existed.

In another case, dailies arrived that included many outtakes (B-negative) that the lab had printed by mistake. During shooting, directors identify the shots that are to be printed (circled takes or A negative), those to be **held** (printed but marked as tentative), and the outtakes, those that are rejected for some reason (B negative.) In this case, the lab had printed the outtakes by mistake. Immediately, we called everyone who had received the dailies and told them that the tapes would be replaced with a correct set of dailies and that these were to be destroyed before viewing. This quick action saved embarrassment all around; no one wants to get negative comments on material that was never meant to be seen.

Other technical problems are more serious and won't go away no matter what changes might be made. Shots might have been overexposed or underexposed. In film, the original negative might have been damaged in the lab. Sound might have static, traffic noise might be ingrained with the dialogue, or there might be audio dropouts or differing levels of sound that are inconsistent between masters and subsequent coverage. When the problems are as serious as these, panic can be heard in the voices on the phone. Reshoots, even individual pick-up shots, can be costly, especially if the production crew has already moved to a new location. The powers-that-be need to know at once if there is a solution that won't upset the film's schedule or budget.

At these times, the editor must immediately investigate all facets of the problem, ascertain the options, and judge whether the problem can be fixed without reshooting. Can the scene with the damaged negative be edited in such a way as to tell the story with existing footage, cutting around the damaged portion? Can a minimal addition, such as an insert, fix the problem? Can the background noise be filtered out, or can the dialogue be replaced in ADR? Can digitizing a particular shot and altering some element fix it? What about blowing up a shot, repositioning it, flipping the image, running something backwards, double or triple printing, online fixes, cloning—all the tricks that, while costly, are far less expensive than reshooting? Quite often, only the editor can determine whether it will be possible to fix the problem by spending little or nothing by manipulating the print or a lot of money by reshooting. At these times, a lot rides on the editor's knowledge and experience.

CHAPTER

12 The First Assembly

Perhaps the gods have smiled, and none of the problems catalogued in Chapter 11 have occurred, or—more likely—they have been successfully dealt with. With a sigh of relief, the editor gets down to the actual work of putting the show together and begins to make a *first assembly*.

When assembling a scene for the first time, the editor selects the footage to be used from the various takes of the various shots the director has circled for consideration. This matter of **shot selection** is a critical first step. Proper shot selection is like laying the foundation for a house; the strength and stability of everything that follows depend on it. Most important, proper shot selection can literally shape and improve an actor's performance, eliminating awkward or inferior moments. It can also show the DP's work to best advantage and thereby enhance the visual impact of the film.

Shot selection is the first truly creative step in the editing process and is one of the most intuitive. Most editors will trust their first impressions of the shots that stand out as special; a particular glint in an actor's eye, a telling reaction, an effective camera move—anything that might make a shot especially good. It might not eventually be possible to use the shot, but the editor keeps it in mind and perhaps even begins building around it. Most important, the usefulness of each shot in telling the story of the scene is evaluated, and sometimes visually inferior shots are chosen above others because of their importance in the evolving story.

The shots to be used having been selected, the editor begins to assemble those shots into flowing moments, beats, and scenes, using his or her sense of the story as a guide. Every story moves by the actions and reactions of the characters to one another and to the world of the story, and the editor begins by roughing out the sequence of the evolving event of the scene, using his or her sense of timing to make each cut. An experienced editor can quickly achieve a good first draft of each scene as it comes into the editing room.

Of course, the ability to edit and trim a scene so that the end result is seamless depends on the coverage supplied by the director. However, seldom can a director take the time to do full coverage, and in any case, most prefer to shoot exactly what they want with just enough additional coverage to protect themselves in case they feel the need to make cuts or changes later.

When the first assembly of a scene reveals some sort of problem, such as being too slow or too expository, the editor will assemble it as it was shot and then try to solve the problem in a second version. It's wise to share this version with the director as soon as possible, by sending a copy of it to the set on a tape marked "For Director's Eyes Only." It is important that problems be discussed while the director is in close proximity to the location where the scene was originally shot; this makes it much easier to obtain any needed **pickup** shots. Even if the company has left the location, it is not always necessary to return to the original site for a pickup shot; as long as the actors are still available, it's possible to "cheat" pickups by keeping them tight and using a background similar to the original.

Sometimes, however, the editor discovers that the scene simply cannot be assembled well without trimming or altering it, but in order to cover the edits and maintain continuity it needs some cutaways or **bridging shots.** I remember an example from a party scene in which two actors walked and talked from one part of the room to another; the director had shot **in one,** that is, in a single, flowing master shot. It began with a close shot on a small band as they played their instruments; after a few beats, the camera pulled back to a full shot, revealing the entire set and the two actors moving through the crowd. Having established the geography of the scene, the camera pushed into a tight two shot and moved with the two actors around the room until the end of the scene. Unfortunately, the scene was tedious and boring. I realized that it contained only one important piece of story information, and so it might be possible to trim it effectively; however, there was only one printed take of the flowing master and no coverage. Few options were available; cutting unimportant lines would "jump" the actors from one part of the room to another (a viable choice in a more adventurous film, but this was network television). There was one workable solution: to start the scene later in the take so that it began with the full shot, moved into the actors, and then cut several nonessential lines of their dialogue. These cuts were covered by using the close shot of the band (stolen from the unused head of the take) so that the band footage became the needed bridging shot.

Although this solution worked, if it hadn't, there would have been time to consult with the director and request that a suitable bridge or **cutaway** be picked up, possibly as an insert of party bystanders. Yet another option would have been to omit the entire scene and add the essential story information to another scene, yet to be shot. Sometimes an important line of dialogue can even be inserted into a previously shot scene by using an ADR line.

Editing for Stock Footage and Visual Effects

Sometimes, there is an intentional gap in a scene in which a piece of **stock footage** is to be inserted later. For example, a film that is shot in Toronto might depend on stock footage of the White House to establish Washington, D.C., as the location. Finding and selecting such footage from the offerings of the various **stock houses** can be very time-consuming and is usually left to the assistant editor. Until the proper footage is found, the editor will usually cut a black slug into the film with a title that explains the missing shot.

Editing animated films or movies that rely on CGI graphics presents many interesting challenges. In these situations, the editor is given dailies in which the actors perform in front of a green or blue screen, as explained in Chapter 7. Later, an optical or digital house will remove the neutral green or blue backgrounds and replace them with animation, digitally enhanced backgrounds, or CGI images. The editor normally cuts such incomplete scenes with the aid of storyboards that show the intended composite. The storyboards may be subject to some degree of change, so once the director views these incomplete scenes in the first assembly and they have been adjusted to his or her liking, the sequences are then sent to an optical or digital house such as Disney Animation or George Lucas's Industrial Light and Magic. There, the new backgrounds and elements are integrated into the final cut of the film.

For example, I recently edited a television film that was to take place on the British ocean liner *QE2*. Eighty percent of the story was going to be filmed onboard as the ship sailed across the Atlantic. When I arrived on location in Australia, however, I was told that there had been a change of plans. The *QE2* was no longer available, and the film was now going to be shot on a set that was being constructed on a sound stage using huge green screen backdrops! A few years ago, I would have laughed at this idea, but two months later, I ran the film with the director, fine-tuned it, and turned it over to the Australian digital and optical wizards. Within a week, the first of the newly composited scenes, with the Atlantic Ocean now in the background, began to arrive in the editing room. The transformation was amazing, and the illusion of being at sea was remarkable.

The Rough Cut

As the scenes accumulate, a clear outline of the show as a whole begins to form. An interaction begins between individual shots, scenes, and sequences as the whole begins to form, so that specific choices are informed and adjusted by the emerging overall picture and vice versa. By the time the shoot has wrapped, the editor can soon provide the director with a solid **first assembly** of the entire show, sometimes called a **rough cut**.

Before showing the director the rough cut, however, the editor might, after making a copy of the complete assembly for future reference, take a few days to produce an **editor's cut.** The difference between an editor's cut and a first assembly can be substantial. In the editor's cut, the editor, using his or her experience, sense of pace, and sense of storytelling, has endeavored to achieve the best possible film out of the material at hand. In the most trusted of editor-director relationships, the editor will now use his or her best judgment and eliminate extraneous dialogue, along with scenes that don't seem to contribute to the story or the emotion of the piece, and will set a rhythm for the film that he or she believes suits it best. The editor will usually enhance this cut with some preliminary temporary music and sound effects that complement the film's mood and genre.

The editor's cut, of course, is shown *only* to the director. It can stimulate the director to see some scenes and even the film itself in new ways and can encourage an approach that he or she might never have otherwise imagined. Unfortunately, with the exception of a few theatrical features, it is rare for an editor to be allowed the extra time required to produce a true editor's cut. Most often, the director receives a plain vanilla first assembly a few days after principal photography is wrapped.

The first assembly will sometimes—nearly always—reveal problems, even fundamental flaws in the film. The flaws that may be evident now were not easily foreseen during the first making, when the script was written and developed. Nor were these flaws obvious during the second making, the piece-by-piece process of shooting, as careful as the director may have been. Only now, when the film can be seen in its entirety, and the third making is underway, have the problems revealed themselves for the first time. The most common problems to become obvious at this time are matters of structure, pace, flow, continuity, clarity, internal logic, or dramatic development. If the problems are severe, this can be the lowest point in the director's entire creative process, a devastating experience. The director may need the editor's moral support and reassurance that the show will change and improve, and that these problems will be solved.

It is one of the mysteries of filmmaking that a production can start with a near-perfect script, one in which every scene and every line of dialogue has been worked over time and time again by the writer and director and, in the world of television and studio pictures, also by teams of executives and producers. Then, during shooting, the scenes are rehearsed, and take after take is done to achieve the best possible result. Yet once the film is assembled, many of these same scenes and lines suddenly seem awkward or unnecessary. How is this possible? How does it happen in film after film? The answer, paradoxically, is good directing and good acting. Under the director's guidance, a good actor can convey the meaning of an entire speech with a single look, a gesture, or simply a moment of silence. The written word becomes redundant and should be cut so that what started out as a good literature can end as good cinema. If we could foresee this outcome better and plan accordingly, tens of thousands— sometimes even hundreds of thousands—of dollars could be saved.

The first assembly contains every scene and line of dialogue that was shot, including any impromptu bits of action and dialogue that the director added on the set. Ideally, the assembly will be significantly longer than the final target length of the film. This is because one of the main strategies of editing is the process of *elimination,* of cutting extraneous scenes, lines, even frames of film. This aspect of editing sometimes reminds me of Michelangelo's description of cutting away bits of the stone until the angel lurking within is revealed. Trim, trim, trim, and with each correct trim, pace, clarity, and drama are enhanced. "Less is more," as they say, as long as it is the *right* less.

Most painful are the times when the first assembly runs short, as sometimes happens in television movies for which schedules and budgets are inadequate. The problem now is to artificially extend the running time of the film to fill the required time slot. The editor is, in this case, required to make something out of nothing, but, as

Shakespeare's King Lear says, "Nothing will come of nothing." Equally painful, however, are those more common situations in which the film turns out to be much too long. In television, it might not fit the required time slot; in theatrical features, the studio or the distributor might feel that it is too long to permit three showings during peak evening hours. There have been legendary battles between directors and studios over the length of films, such as the campaign waged by Terry Gilliam to retain the last twelve minutes of his film *Brazil* or the precious minutes that Sir Richard Attenborough was forced to cut from his *Chaplin,* cutting that he believed harmed the film irreparably. When cutting for length, an experienced editor might be able to salvage a scene for its visual value, dropping the dialogue and making a shortened version into a musical montage that enhances the story that is being told. But sometimes perfectly good scenes have to be omitted; these are often replaced later for the video rental or DVD of the film and proudly advertised as "never before seen," or as "the director's cut."

As many changes as may be made as editing proceeds, the first assembly is held as an invaluable reference. Weeks after the editor and the director have reshaped the film, they can return to the assembly and review their changes. Often, a piece of action, a few lines of dialogue, or an entire scene will be reinserted into the cut. The first assembly also helps the producer to reacquaint himself or herself with the film as it was originally photographed. There are times when the director and the producer differ on what lines or scenes should or should not be retained in the film, and the first assembly gives them a ready reference for their discussion.

Editing for the Story

Telling the best possible story is always an editor's primary concern. The choices that are available to the editor in doing this necessarily depend on the material supplied by the director. Ideally, the director will have provided a multitude of choices, having shot the scene with full coverage. This would consist of a **master shot** giving a good view of the set and with almost all of the dialogue and action visible; in addition, there is **coverage** in the form of medium shots, over-the-shoulder shots, POVs, and **close-ups** from different angles and in different **shot sizes** (see Figure 12.1). Most of the time, however, the director will have had time to shoot only a few **angles,** such as a master shot and a few close-ups for coverage. Some directors even try to "edit in the camera" by shooting so that only one way of assembling the scene is possible.

In television, there might be yet another limitation on the editor's choices: Some producers of one-hour shows insist on an editing formula that gives their shows a consistent style. For example, early in my editing career, I worked for QM (Quinn Martin) Productions and edited a number of television shows with that company, shows such as *The FBI, Streets of San Francisco,* and *Banyon.* All of these shows had an editing formula that was set in stone by the executive producer, Quinn Martin. Every act opening had to start with an exterior **establishing shot** to set up the locale, and every scene had to start with the master shot and then gradually begin to use closer coverage as the

SIZE OF SHOT

Possibly the most elementary decision that the director makes is the size of shot. At each precise moment of a scene how close is the subject to the lens? How much is included in the frame? How much is left off screen?

It is a decision about 'content'. The director must decide on the meaning of the image at this instant. The point of 'proxemics' theory is that the camera -- as imaginary observer -- has a psychological attitude to the character, a feeling very clearly defined by the distance between the subject and the lens.

The closer we (the camera) are to the performer, the greater the 'empathy'. The further away we are the more we are 'objective', disinterested, uninvolved. Increase in shot sizes creates a rise in tension: a decrease relaxes our feelings of participation.

D.W. Griffiths said "the camera can photograph thought." Moreover, it does so in a double sense. At very close quarters, the camera can scrutinise the unspoken and internal feelings of thought that are 'betrayed' by the eyes. But, at the same time, the shot size (as well as the editing) makes a statement about the director's thoughts and feelings about the subject.

LONGSHOT. Figure is too far away to hear conversation or to see facial expressions.

MEDIUM LONGSHOT. Figure is 'theatrical' scale as on stage. Performance is projected.

B.C.U.
CLOSE UP
CLOSE SHOT
MEDIUM CLOSE SHOT
MEDIUM SHOT
LONGSHOT

MEDIUM SHOT. Hip length. A conversational level of exchange. The literal sense of words balanced with 'non-verbal' meanings.

CLOSE SHOT. Head and chest. More personal. Feelings and thoughts are visible and carry as much weight as the meaning of the dialogue.

CLOSE UP. Head only. More 'interior' feeling. Dialogue may now be less significant than 'subtext'-the things that are not verbalized.

BIG CLOSEUP. Eyes and mouth now 'betray' the things words cannot say. As an image size, it is 'too close for words'.

FIGURE 12.1   Shot Sizes. This material was written and drawn by the late Alexander Mackendrick, director of such films as *The Man in the White Suit, The Ladykillers,* and the Academy Award–winning film *The Sweet Smell of Success.*

scene reached its crisis. Even in a scene in which the opening line was extremely important, we still had to use the opening establishing shot first, then "pop in" to a close-up for impact. As restrictive as it was, this formula was very successful and worked well for many years, as it still does today in many other TV shows. But it was frustrating to a young editor who wanted more freedom and the chance to break the rules in order to be more creative.

Thankfully, tastes have changed. Today, there are fewer rules or formulas governing the way editors endeavor to tell a story. But as the old formulas have given way to greater freedom, the temptation to make flashy cuts, to edit in a way that calls attention to itself, has increased. It is still the editor's responsibility to use the new freedom effectively for the sake of the story, to fulfill the emotion, meaning, and dramatic structure in each scene. To do this, the editor must first survey the available footage and identify the shape of the action within the scene, saving the most dramatic shots, especially the closer angles, for use at the most important storytelling points.

Here's a simple example. The following speech is the emotional climax of a scene in which a sixteen-year-old daughter is telling her mother that she is leaving home:

DAUGHTER: I think you're missing the point, Mother! I love David and I'm leaving home to move in with him whether you like it or not! There's nothing you can do to stop me.

We have two shots to choose from: a close-up of the daughter and another of the mother. As we begin to edit the scene, we must ask ourselves, what is really happening here? Who is the scene most about? Let's imagine three different contexts. In the first, the scene is about the daughter finally asserting her independence from her mother. Read the speech with that understanding, and ask yourself on which lines, if any, you would cut away to the close-up of the mother? In this case, I suggest that no cuts are needed, and we should hold on the daughter's close-up throughout. In fact, cutting away to the mother would dilute the action.

Now imagine another context for the same speech. Here, the scene is mainly about the change in the relationship of mother and daughter. How would you edit it this time? In this context, we will want to see the effect of the daughter's action on her mother. Therefore, I would cut to the mother immediately after "I love David" in order to see her pained reaction as the daughter's hurtful words hit home. I would stay on the mother, overlapping the following line—"I'm leaving home to move in with him whether you like it or not"—then cut back to the daughter as she delivers her final line, "There's nothing you can do to stop me." In this version our focus is on the relationship, rather than on one character or another, so we spend an almost equal amount of time on each.

We might even imagine a third context in which this scene is mainly about the mother and her reaction to losing her daughter. In this case, the mother's reaction is of greater interest than the daughter's action, and we might well stay on the mother and overlap the daughter's lines throughout.

As simple as these examples sound, there is more involved than simply making the edits. The rhythm and flow of the scene must also be considered. We might cut to the mother for a silent reaction after "I love David," thereby creating a pause in the daughter's speech. This might or might not cause a disruption in the pattern of the daughter's speech or the flow of the scene, depending on the duration of the silent cutaway. Or we might make the cuts at moments that work *against* the rhythm of the lines to create greater tension. How does an editor know at what moment to cut away and how much time to allow for the cutaway before and after the overlapped line? This is where a sense of rhythm, pacing, and experience come into play and where the art of editing unfolds into the art of storytelling.

Here's another example of using a simple deletion to enhance the storytelling process. I recently edited a scene in which a young female detective, standing next to her boyfriend, received a phone call with the following news regarding her partner:

FEMALE DETECTIVE: (answering cell phone) Yes, it is. (reacts in horror) Oh, my God! Teddy? (beat) I'll be right there!

BOYFRIEND: What is it?

FEMALE DETECTIVE: Teddy's been shot. He may not make it.

I suggested that we end the scene right after "I'll be right there!" and thereby drop the last two speeches. Leaving out the information about Teddy being shot added suspense and helped to propel us forward to the next scene, in which the female detective arrives at the crime scene and the viewer discovers that her partner has been shot, which is now new information. Simple trims and deletions like these help to develop dramatic tension and keep the story moving. Less is indeed often more.

It is sometimes—not always—effective to break the rules of editing. One such rule is *crossing* or *jumping the line,* sometimes called *crossing the x/y axis.* Crossing the line is a term that denotes a mistake in the eye-line of actors. For instance, if two actors are facing each other in a conversation, the single shot of each should have them looking in the correct directions (one to the right, the other to the left) and at the same angle off the lens (away from the centerline of the frame.) If the camera is set up incorrectly, the actors will not seem to be looking at each other. (If such a mistake has been made, careful editing can sometimes help to minimize it by using footage in which the actors are looking up, down, or somewhere in between or by cutting away to an onlooker or some other shot.) Crossing the line is one of the last rules I break because it is so disorienting, and editing that is distracting to the narrative of the story is seldom useful—unless it is serving a point. In a famous example, Alfred Hitchcock chose to literally jump the line in his famous crop duster sequence in *North by Northwest.* At the moment when Cary Grant leaps into a ditch to escape an attacking airplane, the camera suddenly "jumps" 180 degrees to a reverse angle (see Figure 12.2). Such moments can be very effective, and editors are free to break rules in their quest to tell the best story as well as possible according to the director's vision.

Editing for the Actor's Performance

Sometimes beginning directors and editors try to correct problems in ways that actually make them worse. For example, when faced with an emotional scene that feels lethargic, the editor might try to improve the pace by tightening up all of the dialogue, reducing to a minimum the pauses between lines. This is a mistake because it treats symptoms without considering their cause, treats externals with no regard for internals. When the dialogue has been tightened to such an extent that there is no longer room for dramatic looks or pauses, the internal logic and psychological reality underlying the scene are destroyed. The editor must remember that what we see characters do or say comes from inner psychological processes that must be respected. There are, in fact, two levels of action, the external and the internal, which must feed one another. Every good actor knows this, and the editor must know it too. In fact, the seemingly lethargic scene might be suffering from a lack of continuity of this underlying psychological action and might actually benefit from having cuts extended, with added frames of film that allow the actors time to react and think, allowing the emotion in the scene to build to its proper climax. Once the audience is caught up in this

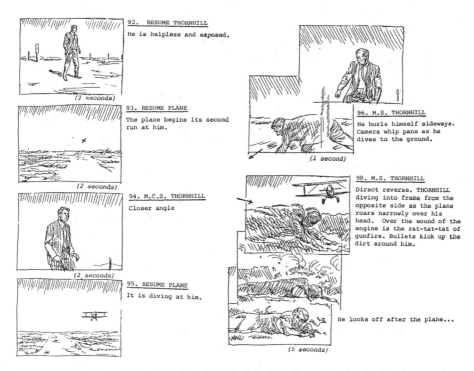

FIGURE 12.2 **From Alfred Hitchcock's *North by Northwest*.** Again, the drawings are by Alexander Mackendrick.

psychological flow, the film no longer feels slow but becomes magnetic in its power to hold our attention.

There is no better way to edit a scene than by locking onto a good actor's performance. When it's working, stay with it as long as the drama holds, and don't cut away just because his or her line of dialogue is over; delay the cut into the silence that follows or the silence in which a reaction is being formed by the listener. Some of the strongest emotions on film are experienced during these silent moments, when we are focused on the internal processes of a character's mind. I watch for these golden moments when screening dailies; they are usually found in the actors' eyes.

Sometimes, however, an actor needs an editor's help. If the performance is timid or, conversely over the top, if it is erratic or, conversely monotonous, the editor can actually "give" an actor a performance through careful shot selection, sometimes even going back to the B negative to find good moments, borrowing shots from various takes or even from other scenes, avoiding awkward moments by cutting away, selecting only the best dialogue and piecing it together under other shots, and using a number of other tricks. At such times, the editor is helping not only the actor but also the entire show.

Editing Action

Action sequences, such as car chases, fights, battles, and explosions, present special challenges for the editor. The first challenge is the sheer volume of film involved. Because action sequences are costly, difficult, and even dangerous to stage, most directors will shoot a tremendous amount of coverage in hopes of avoiding a second take. The editor is inundated with roll after roll of dailies, and it is a mind-numbing task to sort through it all. But we are thankful for this mass of film, because the more coverage the editor is given, the better the action sequence can be. Editing action is, by its very nature, a matter of trial and error. The key is to find the best of the best footage and set it aside. In reviewing this much smaller group of selected takes, the action sequence begins to come into focus, and a through-line begins to emerge and take on a life of its own. The editor can then proceed to start assembling the sequence.

Unfortunately, as much film as may have been shot, when the whole is assembled, there might be bits and pieces missing, causing gaps or awkward transitions in the action. With little or no chance for a total **reshoot** because of the enormous cost, the editor is called on to save the day. Sometimes a few inserts of limited details can be reshot; cutting away to the reactions of characters or onlookers is always a good way to cover an awkward cut or fill a hole, and these can be relatively inexpensive **reshoots** (although I often suggest that directors shoot such potential cutaways during the principal shoot). Of course, any reshoot, however modest, is an expense, and there might be simpler and more inventive solutions.

For example, I have worked on several action sequences in which I've had to use the same piece of film over and over, making it look different each time through a variety of techniques. I might flip the shot to create a reverse image or run a section of film backwards to reverse the direction of movement. A bit more expensive, but more flexible, is turning the shot into an optical, that is, having a specialty laboratory put the shot into an optical printer, where it can be manipulated, frame by frame, in a variety of ways. If the film has sufficient resolution to withstand enlargement without becoming grainy, I might have it blown up, thus turning a wide shot into a closer shot or a medium shot into a close-up. Once enlarged, the shot can also be repositioned within the frame. The optical printer can also tilt the frame one way or the other to alter its perspective.

A similar technique is to have the shot digitized, that is, to have each frame of the shot scanned electronically and converted into a digital record. Once it is digital, almost unlimited alterations can be made. Colors can be altered with ease, and elements can be added or removed. I once had to erase a very large bus from the background of a shot to restore continuity in a scene. Digitizing film is currently an expensive proposition, though the price is dropping steadily as technology advances, and shows that are shot on film are often digitized directly from the original negative. A show that is shot digitally in high-definition 24-frame digital video is, of course, at a tremendous advantage when the editing process requires that the image be manipulated. There is almost nothing that can't be done in the virtual world of digital.

13 Toward a Locked Cut

The first assembly (and the editor's cut, if any) having been carefully reviewed, the editor and director now set out to prepare the *director's cut*. This will be the film as the director intended it, but unless the director has the rare and precious right of final cut in his or her contract, this cut will be delivered to the producer, whereupon significant changes are likely to be demanded. But for now, the editor and director set out to fulfill the director's plan during shooting.

The rules of the Directors Guild of America (DGA) guarantee to the director a period of time during which he or she may work in private with the editor before anyone else is permitted to see the result. In television, the time is short; sitcoms are edited in a day or two and episodes of one-hour television series receive only a few days more. In fact, many TV directors move on to new projects after seeing only a rough assembly and giving a few notes; they know that the show's producers will have the final say about editing in any case. For a standard made-for-television movie, the director is given ten days of private editing time and although his or her work is taken seriously, the network may recut the picture after the director has left the project. For a high-quality cable film, twenty days is allowed, and the cable companies tend to treat directors with greater respect, making changes only with the director's participation. In theatrical films, a minimum of six weeks is allowed for the creation of the director's cut, and directors at this level are treated with great respect, though only a few enjoy the right of final cut. All these guidelines can be shortened or lengthened in special circumstances by negotiation with the DGA.

The Director's Cut

As the director's cut is created, the editor and director essentially must recreate the storytelling process with the actual elements now before them. In the case of independent films, the script has often evolved as shooting has progressed. In television and studio films, the established script, as approved before shooting by the network or studio, has been the bible that everyone has followed throughout the shoot, although some changes may have been approved along the way. But in both worlds, now that shooting is complete, the intention, values, drama, and meaning of the story must be recreated as the editor and director look at the actual footage and begin anew to shape the scenes, the sequences, and the overall film.

The work begins with a thorough review of the first assembly or editor's cut. The director makes notes of what he or she likes or dislikes about it, and a discussion ensues. The editor now has an opportunity to explain some of his or her choices and even to show the director the rejected alternatives. Why was one take used instead of another, or why was a cut made as it was? Sometimes it's a matter of matching, as when the rhythm of a performance differs between master and coverage or there is a problem in matching the physical position or business of the actors. Sometimes lines of dialogue have been altered, transposed, or overlapped, making it impossible to cut at a desirable point. Perhaps an otherwise excellent shot has been marred by soft focus or has been overexposed or underexposed. Once the director understands the options that are available, given the reality of the shot footage, the editor and director begin to make changes.

Most of the changes the director will request usually have to do with timing and placement of cuts, the overall rhythm of scenes and of the film itself, enhancement of performances through different shot selections, transposition of scenes, and trimming or even omitting scenes entirely. The work proceeds scene by scene, then sequence by sequence, and finally the entire show is screened several times over to judge its overall pace and timing.

On some occasions, the editing process will actually extend, alter, or even depart from the intention of the established script in a particular scene or even in larger ways. In this sense, editing can be a kind of rewriting of the show, a true "third making." This happens when the director or the actors have given their personal creative energy to the show in a way that has altered its content from what was on the written page. They have created a new cinematic reality. It is up to the editor to recognize this new reality in the dailies and to incorporate and shape it into the evolving life of the project. Editing a scene, a sequence, or an entire film that has come to life in the camera in a way that transcends its life on the written page is a wonderful experience, one that is well worth pursuing.

Directors often want to enhance their cut with **temporary** (temp) **music and sound effects,** some of which the editor might have already provided. Temporary music and effects can be important in setting the mood and emotional content of the film and can even act as a guide for the composer and the sound department. With the surprisingly good sound-mixing capacity of most modern editing systems, music and sound effects can be "borrowed" from CD's, albums, and other sources. This early "temped" version of the film might be sent to the composer and sound department for their first review of the picture so that the composer can begin creating themes and the sound department can begin its sound design. The sooner the composer and the sound department are involved, the better the final sound track has a chance to be. In fact, every so often, one or more pieces of temp music will turn out to be so perfect that the rights to the original will be purchased for use in the final version of the film. However, some composers object to temp music, feeling that it impinges on their creativity (more on this in Chapter 16).

A further component of the director's cut is the **main title sequence.** The contractually approved copy for the opening titles usually does not arrive in time for the editor to lay out the main title for the first assembly. The legal department, which is bound by the rules of various unions, guilds, and the various individual deal memos, usually doesn't give final approval to the title copy until it's time for the director to deliver the director's cut, or even later. Aware of this delay, the editor asks for an unapproved main title list from the producer and uses it to rough out the main title credits, superimposing title cards (anywhere from twelve to twenty-eight or so) over opening backgrounds. Supported by temp music, these temporary credits (which are usually fairly accurate) gives the director's cut a proper opening and helps to give a sense of the overall length of the film.

The preparation of the director's cut can be both exciting and frustrating. As in any creative process, new ideas are always evolving. The director might wake up one morning with a totally new concept for a scene or sequence. As any director will attest, there are moments, even scenes, in almost every feature film, made-for-television movie, or series episode that were unscripted and have been created in the editing room.

The Producer's Cut

The relationship of director and producer has a profound influence on the editing process. In an independent film, the producer has usually helped the director bring the film to fruition and is an ally. In television and studio situations, the producer has developed the project, participated in hiring the director, and has worked with the director during the Shoot but owes his or her final allegiance to the financing entity rather than to the director. The possibility of disagreement exists in both situations, but it is best for a film if the director and the producer work closely together. The director might even invite the producer into the editing room before delivery of the director's cut. This can have many advantages, especially on a tight schedule. The director and producer can air their differences early, while there is still time to compromise and come up with workable solutions that will satisfy both. Also, the producer might have special knowledge that is useful in making choices, having usually been working on the story far longer than the director—for weeks, months, or even years. If all goes well in this way, the director's cut will also reflect the ideas of the producer. When the producer has not been involved in the creation of the director's cut, however, he or she (or they) might suggest changes in the director's cut to create a **producer's cut.**

Assuming that the producer has not participated in the creation of the director's cut, it's not unusual for the producer to suggest changes. He or she may have discovered important lines of dialogue or story points that have been inadvertently omitted. The director and the editor have recut the film several times, and they know the story so well that they might have begun to make assumptions, forgetting what a first-time viewer will need to understand the film. Sometimes these omissions need only the slight reinforcement of a line or two of dialogue; at other times, a deleted scene might need to be reintroduced.

Some producers might even attempt major alterations in the director's version of the film. A few actually boast that they recut their pictures so extensively that they replace the director, in a sense, as the "real" filmmakers. Be this as it may, the producer might make a number of structural changes to the director's cut in an effort to change the shape or emphasis of the story, to enhance or diminish certain performances, or to achieve a certain overall length. When this happens, scenes are used as "musical chairs" and are moved, trimmed, deleted, reinstated, or deleted again, over and over. Scenes can become the subject of territorial warfare as one or another of the participants fights to assert his or her authority over the film. One director I know purposely leaves a few bad moments, speeches, or even scenes in the director's cut, to give the producer "something to cut." In any case, the producer's cut is soon sent to the studio, network, or other financing entity for final approval, and a whole new phase of the editing process begins with the first screening.

The First Screening

As strong as the relationship between editor and director may be, it faces a major test when the show is screened for the first time by those who will ultimately decide its fate. In student films, it is presented to the faculty. In independent feature or documentary films, it may be presented to a group of investors, potential distributors, or the screening committee of a festival. In television and studio situations, it is screened by studio or network executives, and other interested and influential individuals. In all these cases, this is a difficult time when everything the director and editor have done to that point is on the line. The work is at its most vulnerable point, and feelings can run high.

One of the most common areas of criticism at this first screening is the need to shorten the picture by eliminating some scenes or portions of scenes to achieve improved unity and impact or to conform to a certain required overall length. If done with care and with regard for the director's overall scheme, this culling process can often be an opportunity for great improvement in the film, but if material has survived the initial editing process leading to the director's cut, it will be dropped only with some regret. After all, a lot of thought and effort goes into shooting a scene, and when cuts are made, there is bound to be a certain amount of blood mixed with the film on the cutting room floor.

Fortunately, the choice to delete (*lift*) a scene, a shot, or even a character, is not always painful. Often, the editor and director have already discussed the element more than once and know that it is vulnerable; sometimes they have even made a small wager that it will or won't be cut. At other times, the director knows in his or her heart that the element is superfluous, but is clinging to the understandable hope that everyone will love it after all; in such cases, the director needs only the confirmation of the opinion of others to drop it. But sometimes there are elements in the film that are special in some way to the director, such as a particular location, an actor, an emotional moment, or a particular scene or shot. The director might have lost his or her objectivity about such an element and might fight to retain it, even though it might not be necessary to the film and in fact might slow the film down or distract from its central story or meaning. At these times, a real fight can ensue.

The editor is often respected as an arbiter of such questions, and his or her opinion can sometimes swing the decision one way or the other. This can put the editor in an especially difficult position. When asked whether such an element should be cut or not, the editor must express himself or herself honestly, keeping the good of the picture paramount over personal feelings and political considerations, but with great diplomacy. Cutting a favorite element can be extremely painful. It is said that writer William Faulkner believed that the key to good storytelling was "to kill all your darlings." As difficult as this can be, the editor will ultimately be respected for it.

A special responsibility rests with the editor when a first-time director is hired. In hiring a first-time director, the producers have taken both a career and a financial risk; they may understandably demand and deserve much greater input and watch their fledgling director as closely as a banker watches the accounting ledgers. It's quite common, for instance, for the producers to insist that a first-time director hire a particular editor, usually someone with a proven track record. In such cases, the producers may well expect that the editor will report directly to them, or at least keep them fully informed of what is happening during the shoot; they especially want to know immediately if anything begins to go wrong. This puts the editor in a very difficult position. On principle, an editor owes his or her first allegiance to the director and must do his or her best to protect the person at the helm while still serving the needs of the producers and the film itself. This sometimes requires the wisdom of Solomon.

Focus Groups

In the Hollywood system, differences of opinion among the director, producer, and network or studio executives might be settled by submitting the film to a test audience. In fact, most networks, cable companies, and studios now use these test audiences as a matter of course, even when no disagreements about the show exist, to help provide guidance for the marketing campaign. These test screenings involve what is called a **focus group.**

A focus group is very different from a sneak preview, which may be held later in the production process for a theatrical film. A focus group is a more or less private event, usually conducted by a company that specializes in this type of testing. The group itself usually numbers from fifteen to thirty individuals, chosen to represent the **demographic** (age, ethnicity, income, and educational level) of the potential audience for the film. They are usually paid twenty to thirty dollars to attend and are brought into a small but well-equipped screening theater. After they have filled out an introductory questionnaire, this paid audience, now each and every one a critic, is shown the film, which is usually projected in video with a fully mixed but temporary sound track called a **temp dub.**

Not to be confused with temp music and effects, a temp dub is a complete rendering of the show, a combined effort by the editing department, the composer, and the sound department. It entails cleaning up the dialogue tracks, adding any necessary replacement dialogue, improving the sound effects, and coming up with a temporary music track. It is an extra expense that is avoided for all formats except big cable movies and features.

After the screening, the members of the focus group complete another carefully prepared questionnaire and rate the picture on a scale of 1 to 100, with 100 being best. Then a trained moderator conducts a question-and-answer session that usually lasts about an hour. The discussion can sometimes involve the producer, the director, and studio executives, though usually they merely observe.

The questions that are asked are aimed at finding any weaknesses in the film. A few of the questions normally asked are, did you think the actors were well cast in their parts? Would you recommend the film to your friends and family? What actor or actors stood out? Did you find the story slow? If so, when? Was the story confusing? If so, when? The answers to these questions, even when uncomplimentary or not well thought out, can sometimes give the filmmakers new insights or at least settle questions, such as how best to end the film or whether a subplot is distracting or not. The studio, producer, and director have to read between the lines and not accept all comments at face value. It's up to them to identify the soundest criticisms and, if they believe them to be valid, to make the required changes to improve their film. The changes may be minor, involving some simple recutting, or the changing of some lines by ADR. Or they may be major and involve reshooting some material.

Large-scale reshoots are costly because they are essentially miniproductions, requiring the startup of an office and often the hiring of new personnel, the re-creation of some sets, and the retrieval of costumes, props, and dressing. (It is common practice for unusual costumes, props, and dressing to be held in reserve until the editing process is completed in case a reshoot is ordered.) Of course, reshoots are not always extensive. Sometimes a simple **insert,** such as a character's point-of-view (**POV**) of a prop, can help to explain something that puzzled the audience or can provide a cutaway that hides a gap left by deleted material.

Some producers, such as the legendary David Puttnam (*Chariots of Fire, The Killing Fields*), actually plan on reshoots as a matter of course. Puttnam believed that it was better to shoot more economically during principal photography and then add specific needed material later by "shooting to the cut," as he called it, when shooting could be on a nearly one-to-one basis without waste. In this view, it is as if the main shoot produces a first draft of the film, which is then fulfilled by another modest round of reshoots. This is an interesting way of working and was probably more economically viable in Puttnam's native England than in the United States. In any case, it is not the typical American way of working—at least not on purpose.

Preview Screenings

Preview screenings are different from focus groups. They are larger, more public events and usually occur when the film is at an advanced stage of completion. On rare occasions, television and cable movies are previewed for publicity purposes, but such public previews are relatively expensive and are more often held for feature films, when they are called *sneak previews*. They may be held to determine some unanswered creative question, such as how best to end the film. For example, the feature film *Fatal Attraction*, starring Michael Douglas and Glenn Close, was previewed, and because of many negative reactions to the Glenn Close character being left alive at the end of the movie, the ending was reshot with her being killed. The movie was previewed again, and this time the comments were very positive, and the film went on to become a financial success.

Preview audiences are composed of whomever decides to attend. Control over the selection of the screening audience is achieved mainly through the choice of the theater's location. A teenage comedy such as *Orange County* or a young adult action film such as *The Fast and the Furious* will probably be screened in a location that draws a youthful high school and college crowd. Movies like the darker, sophisticated love story *Monster's Ball* or *Gosford Park*, a film that deals with the social mores of England in the 1930s, will probably be previewed at a big-city art house or in a community that attracts an older, upscale, and more sophisticated audience.

Before a preview screening begins, review cards are passed out to the audience with questions very much like the ones that are asked at a focus group. The main difference is that the preview group members simply fill out their cards on their own and turn them in as they exit the theater. They don't have to worry about how intelligent they sound or have their opinions read aloud in front of their peers, as do those in the more intimate focus groups. As a result, the anonymous response cards from preview screenings usually contain simpler, more honest reactions, some literate and others quite cryptic, such as "Great!" or "What a turkey!"

Some producers put a great deal of emphasis on preview screenings and, as in the example of *Fatal Attraction*, will undertake costly changes on the basis of audience reaction. Of course, such radical changes are rare. More often, preview screenings are used to determine marketing and release strategies or, in the case of studio pictures, whether or not to release the film at all.

Locking the Cut

Once the financing entity has held its focus groups and previews, if any, and everyone has come to an agreement on the final form of the show, we finally have a *locked cut*, meaning that no further changes will be made to its visual aspect. This is necessary so that all the auditory elements of the film can be created and synchronized to the picture with some certainty that the picture itself won't change. Now the wheels are set in motion to produce the final score, the final sound design, and the dub of the film. If changes are made after this point (that is, if the cut is unlocked, as it sometimes is), there may be changes in the length of music cues or sound effect cues, changes in frame reference numbers, and other upsets that cause costly delays.

When the film is locked, the editor will instruct his or her assistants to create another version of the cut that strips out all temporary music and effects so that the composer and the sound effects department will have a clean copy of the film on which to begin work. All temp music and effects will be kept for reference with the original locked version of the film, but now the composer and sound department begin to create original music and sound effects that are composed and designed specifically for the film.

Video copies of the clean locked cut, with time code, are sent to all departments involved in the final working stages of the film. The publicity department will begin work on promotional spots and trailers. The composer will begin writing to the locked time code on the cassette copy. The sound department will finalize their sound design and distribute additional video copies to the dialogue editor, the sound effects editors, the Foley artists, and the ADR editors. If film negative is to be cut, the original negatives, so far untouched since the dailies were transferred, are retrieved from the lab, and the negative cutting process begins.

At any time during the above process, it's not unusual for the producers and/or the studio executives to decide to have just one more screening of the film for a few friends and family members. And, again, it's not unusual for the friends and family members to have opinions on the film, opinions that might require changes. On one such occasion, I was viewing the final corrected answer print of a theatrical film when word came down to us to place a hold on everything. The six hundred release prints were not to be printed. There was going to be a reshoot. The ending of the movie was being changed. Within one frantic, almost sleepless week, during which $600,000 was spent, the new scene was rewritten, the stars and crew were reassembled, and a new ending was shot and edited. The ending of the movie was remixed, the new negative was cut, and a new answer print was made to finalize the picture. Fortunately, the new ending was much better than the old one and helped to make the picture a success. The moral of this story is that a locked picture is *never* locked until it is released and shown to the public.

14 Dubbing, Timing, and Printing

As Bernie Laramie explained in Chapter 8, sound design has become an important element of many films, and the director and editor work with the sound supervisor to ensure its appropriateness to the overall design of the show. The sound supervisor in turn works with the sound designers and editors to prepare the various prelays that will be used in the final mix. These are the many tracks of sound effects (both "hard" and environmental) and the Foley. These prelays appear at the final mix as if by magic, the sound editors usually having done their work in complete anonymity. There are several postproduction sound elements that are added to the dialogue recorded on the set to create the final dialogue track. These are supervised by the director and editor directly, with the cooperation of the sound supervisor. They are all elements involving performances by live actors, mainly ADR, narration, and Walla.

ADR, Narration, and Walla

One of the first steps taken after the film is locked is the preparation of the dialogue track. Using the original production tapes, the sound supervisor or dialogue editor will clean the production sound tracks of all extraneous noises and distracting sounds. He or she will notify the editor if there are lines of dialogue that have to be replaced through ADR (automatic dialogue rerecording, also known as **looping**), a process whereby the original dialogue is removed and replaced by a new recording done on a sound stage.

ADR is necessary when the production dialogue track was ruined in some way. Perhaps there was traffic, an airplane, or other ambient noise; perhaps the editing of the film has made it necessary to adjust the dialogue in the scene; perhaps there was an inaccuracy or flaw in the script that went unnoticed until Post, and a little added dialogue will solve the problem; perhaps rerecording a speech or two will improve the performances.

The ADR editor will make a list of all lines that might have to be replaced and will send this list to the director, the producer, and the editor. They will check each listed line and decide which might be saved by replacing them with lines "stolen" from another take, by actually replacing the take with another, or by having the dialogue editor "clean them up." It's almost always best to go with original dialogue if at all possible, as there is nothing like a good original sound recording.

Once the lines that must be replaced have been identified, a final ADR list is generated (see Figure 14.1). The necessary actors are then called into a special ADR stage, where they "re-act" the performance. The film containing the lines to be replaced are broken into short pieces, and the actors watch them on a large screen. As the section to be replaced approaches, the actor hears three short beeps in an earphone and speaks the piece so as to match his or her mouth movements on the screen, with whatever adjustments in line delivery that may be required.

Several takes are usually necessary to achieve a final result that marries seamlessly with the original production track. Looping is a skill that most actors can quickly learn. For some actors, however, the impersonality of the ADR stage can stifle their powers to recreate their performance; others take to it naturally. The legendary producer John Houseman once told me that Sir John Gielgud, called to loop a very long speech in Shakespeare's *Julius Caesar,* waved away the little pieces of dialogue prepared by the looping supervisor and read the entire speech in one take, synchronizing perfectly to every frame of the film.

Some producers and directors insist that they want to avoid ADR. They claim that they can always tell when ADR is used and that it is an awful technique. They are simply misinformed. The only ADR that is noticeable is ADR that is improperly done. At the final mix or at a dialogue premix, the dialogue mixer will work with the ADR recordings to make them blend imperceptibly into the original production track. If it is done correctly, it cannot be noticed. For an extreme example, watch the splendid movie *Greystoke: The Legend of Tarzan, Lord of the Apes.* This was Andie MacDowell's movie debut, and her Southern drawl seemed out of place against the English accents of the rest of the cast. It was decided to replace *all* of her dialogue through ADR. In an uncredited voice performance, Glenn Close provided the new voice. It was a masterful job, and millions of people have seen the movie, never guessing that ADR was so extensively used.

Narration and voice-overs are also recorded in Post. Narration may come from a character in the film, as in the BBC television miniseries *Brideshead Revisited* or from an omniscient, anonymous voice guiding the viewer through the storyline, as in the feature film *Dune.* Generally, voice-over work is recorded straight, or *dry,* and is then colored during the final mix to fit the overall sound quality of the picture.

The sound supervisor and ADR editor will also program additional background voices that help to give a realistic sound to a filmed location. These additional background voices, such as conversations at a party, the crowd in an airport terminal, the sounds of a hospital, or an audience watching a play, are called *Walla* (a term from the British cinema) and are created by a **loop group,** a company of actors who specialize in background work.

There remains one more major sound element, one that is exceeded in importance only by the dialogue itself, and that is the music or *underscore.* The composition, recording, and preparation of the music for incorporation into the show will be covered in Part Three.

TODD-AO
GLEN GLENN
s t u d i o s
"Miss Evers Boys" HBO-NY
AUTOMATED DIALOGUE REPLACEMENT CUE SHEET

R- 2
1/3/97
Page:_**5**_ of_**27**_

	CHARACTER	START/ STOP	NOTES	CHANNELS 9 10 11 12 13 14 15 16	DIALOGUE
2001.	Douglas	02:00:14:25 02:00:16:20			We'll have to test them first of course......
2002.	Douglas	02:00:16:20 02:00:18:27			Give them wassermans to make sure. I'll take that.
2003.	Brodus	02:00:18:22 02:00:21:10			Doctor, that in itself would be a huge undertaking.
2004.	Douglas	02:00:21:29 02:00:23:25			Great pains for great rewards. Right?
2005.	Brodus	02:00:23:29 02:00:27:20			You don't intend on them they have syphilis do you?
2006.	Douglas	02:00:28:10 02:00:31:04			Well if they have it we'll have to tell them something won't we?
2007.	Miss Evers	02:00:31:23 02:00:35:02			Well, *maybe we better not use a name they never heard before..........*
2008.	Miss Evers	02:00:35:02 02:00:37:01			That'll just scare them off doctor.
2009.	*GROUP*	02:00:37:28 02:01:04:20			(HOSPITAL CORRIDOR WALLA)
2010.	*GROUP*	02:01:04:20 02:02:05:05			(HOSPITAL WARD WALLA)
2011.	Miss Evers	02:01:33:08 02:01:38:07			And that new man that's come in, you check him for a fever every two hours and make sure he don't go spiking on you.
2012.	*GROUP*	02:02:05:05 02:02:16:14			(COURTROOM WALLA)
2013.	Miss Evers	02:02:17:03 02:02:20:27			I've been sent here by... I've been sent here by the.....
2014.	*GROUP* MAN	02:03:09:15 02:03:34:10			(SIGHS & GRUNTS)

FIGURE 14.1 An ADR List. Created by Sound Supervisor Richard Taylor.

The Final Mix

After weeks—sometimes months—of preparation, the locked version of the film is brought to the dubbing stage, and the final mix (technically called "rerecording" or commonly called the "dub") begins. The complexity and duration of the dub vary greatly in different kinds of shows. Normal dubbing time for a half-hour sitcom is one day. A one-hour television drama can take from one to two days. A television movie can take three or four days, while a high-quality cable movie may be allotted ten days or longer, depending on the complexity of the film. A feature-length theatrical motion picture will vary widely depending on the original budget of the film but will have one to four weeks of dubbing. For big action or effect films, the dub can take months.

The dubbing stage is the place where all the auditory elements that have been worked on for weeks and months—the dialogue, music, sound effects, ADR, Walla, and Foley—are brought together and run simultaneously with the locked cut of the show. The various prepared sound tracks containing the required effects and elements for the picture, sometimes numbering into the hundreds, are run on digital audio decks that are connected to a dubbing console. The console, a huge affair with row after row of sliders, switches, and knobs, has control over each individual sound track. The mixers who operate the console can raise and lower the volume of each track as well as employ hundreds of sound modifications to filter, alter, distort, enhance, expand, or contract any given sound.

The picture is run in sync with the sound elements. For a television program, it is viewed on a video monitor; for television movies, it is projected in video on a modestly sized screen; theatrical features are projected on full-size screens or larger. (Major studios have a few dubbing stages that rival the most extravagant movie palaces in their size and opulence.) If the show is projected in video (as most except major features are), the picture has reference numbers appearing in windows, just as in the dailies. If the projection is in film, the reference numbers are displayed separately beneath the screen. The reference numbers allow everyone participating in the mix to discuss and place changes.

The mix is attended by a large group of people that will include the director, producer, editor, network or studio representatives, sound supervisor, and mixing crew, as well as the composer and music editor. There is a sense of etiquette that must be observed if the work is to go smoothly. While everyone may have their say as the mix proceeds, there should be only one person giving instructions to the dubbing mixers, and all communications should be channeled through this one voice. In sitcoms and episodic television shows, this will be the associate or executive producer. In all forms of movies, it will be the director, although occasionally, the editor runs the mix.

The dubbing stage is a place for work, concentration, and attention to detail. Unnecessary conversation distracts the mixers and shouldn't be allowed. It is best to restrict visitors unless they are professionals who understand the protocol. If visitors must drop by, it's best if they arrive just as the dubbing stage is preparing to break for lunch so that they can observe for a few minutes but are not present long enough to cause distractions. Besides, dubbing is highly repetitive work, with cues being run over and over with tiny adjustments, and unless one is directly involved, it can be deadly dull and frustrating.

The most active members of the mixing group are the mixers themselves. Good mixers make it a pleasure to come to the dubbing stage every morning to start the day's work, whereas inferior mixers can cause hair-pulling frustration and a loss of time, money, and quality. Mixers must be chosen with great care; references should be checked and those with whom the mixers have recently worked should be queried about the experience.

The number of mixers working on a film is usually dictated by the budget. Cartoons, sitcoms, and trailers (coming attractions), if they are relatively simple, will normally use only one mixer, working alone in a small mixing room. One-hour television dramas, television movies, and small theatrical films usually employ two mixers. Large animated or action pictures may use three mixers. When there are three mixers, each controls one element of the mix: Dialogue is handled by the lead mixer, who sits at the center of the console, with the music mixer on his or her left and the sound effects mixer on the right. As technology has advanced, the number of mixers has commonly been reduced to two, even on large pictures, with the sound effect tracks split between the dialogue and the music mixer. Under the guidance of the director, the mixers will work to prepare a balanced sound track for the final dub of the film.

One of the most important choices made during a mix concerns the balance of the three main sound elements: dialogue, music, and effects. The sound designer is often the champion of the effects track and, left to his or her own devices, will sometimes willingly obscure dialogue and music. The producer and director, however, are the champions of the dialogue, ensuring that important lines remain clearly audible. The composer, or his or her representative, the music editor, is the champion of the music and resists changes in duration and level that disrupt the musical integrity of the cues, though in spite of such objections changes are frequently made by manipulating or repositioning music cues. (In major features, it isn't unusual for the producer to budget a preview using the composer's original score, knowing that if changes are made as a result of the preview, he or she might have to pay the composer to rewrite another version of score.)

Dubbing a film is a real art. Sound levels are experimented with, enhanced, clarified, magnified, and manipulated to create a single, unified effect that can, at times, be magical. Sound, including the carefully chosen absence of sound, can evoke a physical response, one that can touch our hearts, stir our emotions, and completely enfold us in the lives and world of the characters, shaping and fulfilling the story and heightening the impact of the experience. A successful final mix is never easy to achieve, but it is always a very rewarding experience.

Timing

The last major creative step, whether the film is being finished in film or video, is *color timing*. This can be a confusing process because of the number of varied opinions coming from the releasing company, the network, the producer, the director, the director of photography, or the editor, all trying to have a final say in the look of the film, each with his or her own esthetic. It is therefore necessary that as in dubbing, the color timing process be controlled by one individual, and this person's authority should be established from the very beginning of the process. This person's should be the only voice speaking to the color timer, who makes the actual technical adjustments.

In most television shows, this voice is that of the associate producer or post-production supervisor. In theatrical movies, the postproduction supervisor or editor might supervise, but more likely the DP will be present. Committed cinematographers consider timing to be their special domain, and many have their right to supervise the timing written into their contracts. They care so much about controlling the final look of the film, in fact, that they usually do this additional work without additional pay (though that might soon change). In all cases, of course, the director will give final approval.

In the case of film timing, to save money and time, only key frames from each scene may be shown, in the manner of a slide show, though this is the least effective technique for timing. Usually, a trial print is projected without sound (*mute*). The timing of film stock is a matter of trial and error, trying again and again until the right results are finally locked in. Each time corrections are made, a trial print is struck and rechecked. Problems may be caused by the varying density of the film negative, scratches, and dirt. If the DP has been skillful and the gods are smiling, there might be only one or two trial prints before the final result, the *answer print,* is achieved. Even so, it takes long hours, long days, and sometimes weeks, going over every cut in a show, to complete the timing of a film.

Digital timing is a different world. Digital video technology allows corrections to be made very quickly and with tremendous flexibility; the frame can be divided into zones, or certain areas can be isolated, each of which can be timed separately. For example, we once had to reshoot a scene that had originally been shot on film on a sunny day; scheduling problems forced us to do the reshoot on a gray day. Even though our DP was able to match the lighting on the actors, the sky, which had been bright blue in the original, was dull in the reshoot. No amount of adjustment in the film timing would fix the sky without ruining the rest of the frame, since film timing adjustments affect the entire frame. When the scene was digitized, however, it was simple and quick to isolate the sky and render it a lovely, bright blue.

This capacity of digital timing to produce a more subtle and flexible result is so potent that many movies that are shot on film are being timed digitally. This involves creating a digital intermediate master that is used for the timing. This additional expense can be recouped in larger projects. As *American Cinematographer* says, "The resulting digital master can be used to create not only the 35mm print, but also the VHS, broadcast and DVD masters, which ultimately saves the time and expense of multiple film **transfers**—while also maintaining a consistent, correct look for all markets."[4]

Cinematographers are delighted with the control they gain through digital timing, which makes many special film treatments such as prefogging and bleaching unnecessary and allows unfettered experimentation with the look of the film. Although digital timing is more instantaneous than film timing, it is not in fact faster; the ability to experiment and to control individual zones and elements of the picture requires prolonged hands-on work by the cinematographer. Roger Deakins, A.S.C., B.S.C., spent three months on the Post for the Coen brothers' *O Brother, Where Art Thou?,*

---

[4]Ibid, p. 76.

and Stephen Goldblatt, A.S.C., B.S.C., spent fifteen working days timing HBO's *Conspiracy.*

The Digital Future Is Now

More and more television shows, as well as commercials, are being shot digitally. These are also broadcast digitally, so no film is involved at any point in their history. Even those television shows and movies that are still shot on film are edited digitally and then broadcast digitally, so the original negatives are never used again once they have been transferred to digital dailies. Only theatrical motion pictures and a few cable films continue to be shot and finished on 35mm film. Eventually, even these will be converted to the digital age as technology advances, film and digital become more and more indistinguishable in quality, and more and more video projection systems are installed in theaters. Although there will probably always be a few filmmakers who will resist the digital revolution, the days of film as the primary medium of the movie business are numbered.

This is progress, and it has opened the filmmaking process as never before. The digital age offers boundless opportunities. The editor's tools, with the advent of the digital age, are ever expanding and will continue to offer new and inventive ways to approach editing. A whole new and exciting world is opening up in the film business.

With new tools being developed continuously, editors are entering a world of expanding opportunities that will enhance our storytelling capabilities. It is more important than ever to see and study all kinds of films and to keep an open mind to change and innovation. A career in editing will more than ever be a rewarding, collaborative, and meaningful adventure. Sometimes we have the opportunity to edit wonderful films, at others times the quality of the projects we work on are less than we might hope, but for good or ill, editing gets into one's blood, stirs the imagination, and makes the creative juices flow. If you are considering a career in editing, get ready for a lot of ups and downs in your life, but also get ready for a lot of creative fun. It has been a great career for me, and I heartily recommend it to anyone.

PART THREE

Movie Music

PATRICK WILLIAMS

> *People who make films should understand what music can do for a film, the way they understand the camera, the use of a prop, what the art director does.*
>
> —Jerry Goldsmith, composer[5]

---

[5]Jerry Goldsmith, "The Composer," *Filmmakers on Filmmaking*, edited by Joseph McBride, J. P. Tarcher, Inc., 1983, p. 139.

CHAPTER

15 The Right Music in the Right Place at the Right Time

I moved to Hollywood in 1968 specifically in hopes of composing music for the movies. The inspiration for this move had come from my musical mentor in New York, Marion Evans, who had an excellent collection of movie sound track albums and even some original scores. Thanks to him, I had spent hours listening to classics such as "Cathy's Theme" from *Wuthering Heights* by Alfred Newman; *Forever Amber, Laura,* and *The Bad and the Beautiful* by David Raksin; *For Whom the Bell Tolls* by Victor Young; *The Sea Hawk* by Erich Korngold; *The Best Years of Our Lives* by Hugo Fried-hofer; *The Days of Wine and Roses* by Henry Mancini; and *The Sandpiper* by Johnny Mandel. I idealized these composers and their music. "If I could ever write music like that," I thought, "my musical life would be a success." And so I was off to Hollywood.

When I arrived in Los Angeles, I had a wife and three small children, so finding work was my top priority. Even with the support and assistance of my New York mentor and the new friends I made in Hollywood, it wasn't easy. I finally started getting some appointments, but being new to Los Angeles, I kept getting lost on the freeways. Still, I kept at it. I have to admit that I would never have made it if I hadn't been sustained in these early years by my love, my *passion,* for movies and movie music.

Now, over 150 scores for theatrical and television films and too many years later, I still feel the same way—just as eager for the next one, just as excited when I put that new tape of a locked cut in the machine for the first time. Very few experiences in my life can compete with the thrill of completing a score and then seeing it work on many levels, emotional as well as technical. I am, however, much more realistic and experienced about the demands and pressures of composing. There are times when it can be terribly frustrating and times when the obstacles prove to be insurmountable. The joy of successful completion is sometimes replaced by the sheer relief of getting the damn thing out the door. In fact, I don't think there is a creative person in the film industry who, at some point in a long career, isn't bitten by the bug of cynicism and thinks about packing it in and finding some form of employment that is more appropriate for a sane adult.

As frustrating as it sometimes is, however, there are special qualities about composing for movies that you don't find in any other branch of the music business. One is the chance to work with fascinating, talented people who feel as excited and passionate about their work as you do. Concert music is essentially composed alone; movie music is a collaboration. Another thing I enjoy is that movie music serves a larger artistic purpose. Concert music must stand on its own; movie music is part of a larger whole and in most cases is not meant to be heard out of context. (Concert versions of classic movie music are usually rearranged adaptations of the main theme or a pastiche of cues; very rarely is a film cue, as it existed in the film, played in a concert format.) Because it is not meant to stand alone, some composers dismiss film music as merely "utilitarian" and therefore impure, calling it "music by the foot." I find this very quality enlivening and exciting. I revel in the total impact of a good film of which my music is a part.

Music is an integral part of our emotional and social lives. It is performed at almost every meaningful human ceremony: weddings, funerals, graduations, parades, and so on. It is also part of our storytelling heritage; the oldest drama in Western culture, the Greek tragedies, were accompanied by music, and the stories told by medieval troubadours were told musically. Even before the movies learned to speak, they were accompanied by music. In life and in the movies, music can heighten experience, create an emotional ambiance, and make us feel elated or depressed, inspire dread or foster hope, arouse suspense, or heighten a climax. At those perfect moments when music and event coincide, they can fuse inextricably into the fabric of experience and stir us to the depths of our souls in a way that nothing else can.

I had a memorable experience of the potential synergy of music and event a few years ago when I entered a cathedral in Florence in midafternoon. A sign outside read, "Organ Recital Tonight." I went inside this deserted, rather musty place and sat down on a cold marble bench. This was a typical church of the Renaissance period—stone everywhere, beautiful stained glass windows admitting a few faint, deeply colored patches of light into the almost palpable darkness, a ceiling of inestimable height, and practically no cloth, no softness, anywhere. I thought to myself that a recording engineer would say, "This is a really live room." I sat for a time alone in the reverberant silence. Then suddenly, from out of nowhere, an organ rang out with a Bach prelude of enormous power and volume. The music careened off stone walls and whizzed around me as the organist rehearsed, literally moving me like some kind of virtual-reality ride. Contained, amplified, and compounded by the huge marble building, the deep pedal tones invaded my body as if the organist was stepping on my heart with his toe. No dub from the latest Hollywood blockbuster, with total digital surround-sound and all its supertweeters and subwoofers, could reproduce what I was experiencing in that church. The massive organ sonorities and the music itself were the perfect fit in this setting, and their power was overwhelming. "This should be a mandatory experience for any aspiring film composer," I thought, "*the right music in the right place at the right time. Bingo!*"

Early Meetings

The process of composing a score for a theatrical feature, television movie, episodic television drama, or sitcom begins with a first meeting (sometimes several separate meetings) between the prospective composer and the director, the producers, and the studio executives, all of whom are often involved in hiring a composer. This is indicative of how potent the power of film music is understood to be. During this first meeting, sequences from the film might be shown, or the composer might have received a sample of the show prior to the meeting. This is an overall first look in which ideas about the music for the show are exchanged on both sides. Although samples of the composer's work have already been heard, this is sometimes a quasi-audition, as two or more composers may be under consideration for the project at this point. The conversation will be focused on subjects such as mood, tone, pace, and the sheer quantity of music, and the style of music intended. The more specific and more comprehensive this discussion can be, the better.

The problem with such discussions, of course, is that they are an attempt to use words to describe something that is inherently beyond words. Music is essentially a nonverbal art, so it is often difficult for the filmmaker to tell the composer exactly what he or she wants and just as difficult for the composer to describe verbally what he or she has in mind. This problem is especially important in these early meetings, when the music is necessarily discussed in the abstract, without concrete examples. Inevitably, everyone resorts to using analogies: It should sound like so-and-so or be like the music from such-and-such a film or a combination of this-and-that. The composer, who would prefer to think of himself or herself as a unique talent writing truly original music, tries to not feel limited by these analogies and strives to translate them into his or her own terms.

The only thing one can predict about these early meetings is their unpredictability. They can run the gamut from nasty conceptual disagreements on musical approaches to "fishing expeditions" in which no one really has any firm ideas at all. Thankfully, they can sometimes be focused, thoughtful dialogues regarding the overall thrust and style of the score. Whatever they turn out to be, these early meetings are extremely important. This is the time when the composer has the best chance to influence the thinking of all concerned and to move the project in the right direction. Obviously, political as well as musical skills are required for a successful outcome.

Here are some tips for success in these early meetings that I have garnered from hard experience:

■ Listen to all points of view before saying too much, and give yourself a chance to weigh your own ideas before expressing them. Speaking too soon might prematurely commit you to an idea that could turn out to be fatally flawed later, such as "Why don't we try a totally jagged and atonal type score?" or "How about a different theme for each of our three main characters?" These are the kinds of things about which one says later, "It seemed like a good idea at the time."

■ Avoid details. Keep your attention on the big picture, which is the overall musical approach to the film. Specifics can always be dealt with later.

■ When someone presents an idea, ask questions about it. Be sure you understand. Try not to leave conceptual loose ends dangling like little snakes that can bite you later. By asking questions now, one avoids those later arguments that start with "But I thought you said. . . ."

- If subordinates (minor executives, assistants) are present at the meeting, don't ignore them. They may not be subordinates forever.
- Although these meetings are a hot seat for the composer, one does not have to have an answer for every question. A simple "That's an interesting thought" or "I'll think about that" is often the best answer.
- Try to avoid disagreements or confrontations. Remember that these are early meetings, and things will change and be more clearly delineated at a later date.

Assuming that the composer survives these early meetings and emerges with both the job and a general idea of what is wanted, the next step is for the composer to begin developing his or her own approach; forming ideas about the overall tone, the musical palette, and the rhythmic and harmonic bases of the score itself; and planning how to win early approval of this approach.

Enter the Machine

Before the advent of computer technology, a composer would be called in when a film was in the final editorial phase. A few meetings later, the cut would be locked, and the composer and director would sit down to *spot* the film, deciding where music would occur and what kind it would be (more on spotting later). The composer would then disappear for some length of time, usually four to six weeks. He or she would then suddenly reappear on a scoring stage in front of an orchestra, and the film score would be recorded while the director and producers listened, hopefully, in transports of awe and delight. With a few exceptions, this is no longer the case.

Today, we have a generation of film composers who grew up with computer technology. This reality has dramatically changed the way in which film music is created. It is no longer the private and mysterious process of the composer sitting alone at his or her piano, wearing out pencil after pencil as phrase after phrase is perfected and scratched onto the music paper. For the composer, computer technology, with the use of *samples,* has created a virtual laboratory of both real and synthesized sounds. Accessed through the keyboard of a synthesizer, these sounds are loaded into the computer and manipulated in myriad ways. For some composers, an understanding of computer programs such as Logic and Pro Tools has become a necessary skill. This process has made film music a more collaborative and interactive process, with computer-generated versions of themes and cues bouncing back and forth on CDs between composer, director, and producers.

The music that is composed through this computer process can then be performed by live musicians. First, the composer, or an arranger-orchestrator, writes a musical score from what has been created on the synthesizer keyboard; there are even computer programs that will print out the score automatically. Using this music, the computer tracks are then replaced (*overdubbed*) by live musicians. Alternatively, the synthesizer can produce the actual music directly, which is appropriately called "machine" music as opposed to acoustical or "real" music. The use of machine music greatly reduces the costs of scoring, and though there is a considerable loss of in subtlety and richness, this has been a boon for low-budget productions such as student and some television and independent films. The speed of the computer process has also been useful for producing the great volume of music needed by weekly television shows, from sitcoms to one-hour dramas.

The computer keyboard has therefore largely replaced the piano for many composers, and almost all film scores today are recorded as a mixture of both machine and acoustical elements. Feature films and high-end cable movies and the main themes of high-quality television shows still tend to use large orchestras that are merely augmented by a machine track containing only a few guiding elements, such as percussion or additional strings. For economic reasons, however, many television scores consist mostly of machine music with only a few live instruments and soloists added.

In all, the composer whose musical training and talent are augmented by good computer skills will be able to handle a broader range of projects and to be more versatile in approaches to scoring films.

Dealing with Temp Music

Today's film editors have access to endless libraries of previously written scores and music of all kinds on CDs. This has allowed directors and editors, eager to make a good impression with the first cut they deliver to the producers, to add music (called *temp music*) as part of the initial editing process, usually even before the hiring of the composer. Temp music can be very elaborate and can consume many hours of a director's and an editor's time.

This can create two substantial problems for the composer when he or she eventually joins the project. First, emotional commitments might have been made to music that is supposed to be temporary, not only by the editor and director who chose it, but also by the producers and executives who have heard it, probably many times over; listening to something over and over brings familiarity and some sense of security (although, as one composer opined, "You can get used to cancer, too"). Second, budgetary considerations (especially in cable and television films) were probably not considered when the temp music was chosen. Because the uncompleted film has at this point not yet been made public, there was no need to receive permissions or pay royalties for music that was "borrowed" for the temp score, and the size of the orchestra that produced the temp music was not a consideration. Therefore, a film with a $40,000 music budget can easily have been temped with a $400,000 score! Skilled directors, whether of television movies or feature films, understand that the temp music will not dictate the final score, but nonetheless, it might have created expectations that the composer will find difficult to fulfill.

It is possible, of course, that the temp music is very good. There might even be a temptation to simply rerecord it, perhaps with minor revisions; this is called *ripping off the temp*. However, it is important to remember that the composer is legally responsible for the originality of the music in the score. If it is proved that music has been stolen from a preexisting source, it is the composer who will be sued for plagiarism, not the producer or the director. There are definite legal consequences for plagiarism, and a composer who is tempted to rip off the temp (or other existing music) must think twice.

For all these reasons, some composers absolutely refuse to even listen to temp music and insist on receiving their first copy of the show with all temp music stripped out. This, however, cuts the composer off from a powerful expression of the director's ideas about the music of the film. It is better for all concerned to approach the temp music as a form of preliminary discussion about the music and not at all as a *fait accompli.*

Another good coping strategy is "If you can't lick 'em, join 'em." I try now to get involved as early as possible in the editorial process and to actually supply some of the temp music myself. Because temp music is in some ways a gigantic fishing expedition, why not supply a few fish? This gives me a running start on composing a score I can live with. Besides providing a measure of control, this process has an additional benefit: It allows producers and executives to react to my musical choices early on. I would far rather have cues rejected early, rather than later when I have put many hours of work into completing them.

To facilitate this, I have organized all my existing scores into an accessible library organized by style and emotional categories in which I can find various styles and types of music quickly and judiciously. Categories such as "suspense," "love themes," "action," and "danger," to name a few, allow immediate reference. This is tremendously useful, and I would encourage any beginning composer to assemble his or her original music into such a library. This is also useful in assembling demo CDs for specific job opportunities. It also provides ideas for later scores, just as sketchbooks help an artist to develop techniques and concepts for finished works.

The Composer and the Film Editor

The film editor can be the composer's best friend or, conversely, his or her worst nightmare. The editor has an advantage over the composer from the outset: The relationship between a director and editor is usually strong and of long standing. Directors tend to trust their editor's instincts, and by the time the composer arrives on the scene, the director and editor have already spent many weeks developing and temping in many musical choices.

Luckily, I have found that film editors often have an excellent sense of musical pace and style. No one (other than the director) understands every cut and every frame (and every problem) of a film as well as the editor does. I have made it a practice to have private conversations with the film editor as early as possible to establish a candid working relationship. An editor often knows what a director is really looking for, often more clearly than the director does. Once, after I had started on a particular film and had begun to reconcile myself to the approach indicated by the temp music, the editor (with whom I had worked before) took me aside and said, "Don't get too committed to this approach. The director's still fishing." This insight was a godsend to me. It turned out that the director was not at all committed to the direction indicated by the temp music. If I had gone on assuming that the temp score was what was wanted, I would have missed the opportunity to take an entirely different approach that resulted in one of the best scores I've ever done.

The Music Supervisor

When preexisting music is needed in a show (that is, music that is not to be written by the composer, but taken from material already published), the services of a music supervisor are needed. This specialist will supply appropriate choices for the director and composer to consider and will then make the complex arrangements to obtain the rights to use the music chosen.

The music provided by a music supervisor may take the form of source music motivated by some element of a scene, such as a jukebox or radio playing in the background. In these cases, historical accuracy must be considered along with appropriateness to the scene, and the encyclopedic knowledge of a good music supervisor is essential. Even more demanding are those cases in which a director or composer decides to use recognizable music as an integral part of the show's underscore as a way of establishing a sense of time and place or mood. In such a case, the music supervisor assumes many esthetic duties and will work as a collaborator with the composer.

The negotiation of music rights, which require payments to both the original composer of a song and the particular artist performing the chosen selection, is a complex process. A canny, well-connected music supervisor can save a production considerable amounts of money.

Because music rights are so expensive, lower-budget productions will sometimes ask the composer to write **sounds-like** music; for example, the composer might write music in the style of a particular period and record it with appropriate instruments as part of the show's score. This music will then be filtered during the final mix and inserted in the show as if it were coming from a jukebox or radio. This can save an enormous amount of money in rights and gives the composer the opportunity to determine the musical quality of all the music in the show.

CHAPTER

16 Preparing to Compose

The composer has survived the first meetings and has discussed the music in general terms with the director and the producers. The temp music has been dealt with. Edited sequences of the film and perhaps an early assembly of the entire film have been viewed. The composer has been thinking about it, of course, perhaps making sketches, trying out themes and instrumentations. But at last the word comes: The cut is locked! Now the work begins in deadly earnest. In a screening room or (more likely) in the composer's own workspace, the locked cut is viewed for the first time from beginning to end.

The First Look

When I watch a film for the first time, I prefer to do it alone and—most important— without thinking about the music! I want the story to speak directly to me, to see and hear it with fresh eyes and ears. I want my emotions to be my own, not what someone has told me I'm supposed to feel. I want to meet the characters, get to know them, develop feelings about them. I allow myself a private critical relationship with the film, one that I rarely discuss with anyone else.

After these private moments, it's time to get to work, to start the process. I will take a break, and after an hour or so, I will watch the film again. This time I will have my legal pad ready and will start making notes. How do I feel about the temp music? What is the overall mood and tone of the film? Where are the slow spots? What is working and what is not? My notes will reflect my own analysis of the picture and might or might not be shared with others.

After this second viewing of the film, I might go for a drive. I have no idea why, but I get ideas when I drive. Perhaps it's because I'm not glaring obsessively at a blank page of music paper or pounding the piano into submission looking for a theme. My mind is open and empty. The key is to stay relaxed and receptive. I don't judge any thought that comes as good or bad; I simply go with it and follow it. One idea flows freely into another. They might be simple ideas for solo instruments or the beginnings of short musical phrases. Sometimes a walk, or playing a game, or some other kind of activity will accomplish the same thing, but I prefer a drive in the car. Those who study

116

the creative process will say that while driving, I am keeping my logical, sequential, verbal "left brain" busy and allowing my intuitive, global, emotional "right brain" to do its thing. Whatever the process, this is when I allow my first impressions to simmer in the broth of my musical unconscious, so carefully prepared by years of study, experimentation, and listening.

After my drive, I return to the film and view it yet again, analyzing my initial reactions. I look for a number of things as I analyzing the film more closely: Recurring characters, situations, or issues might present the possibility of recurring themes; the shape of the action, whereby suspense is built, might suggest supporting musical structures. The greatest musical implications, however, come from the emotional thrust of the film, its overall pace, and its style. Let's consider each.

The Emotional Thrust of the Film

A composer must learn to be a "film psychiatrist." Films are full of emotions and feelings, and nothing goes to the heart of emotions like music. During these early viewings, I ask myself, what is the overall emotional tone of the film? At the most basic level, is it comic or tragic? *The Pink Panther* films are little masterpieces of comedy film scoring. Henry Mancini used clever tunes and interesting textures to maximum effect, yet the music remains transparent, never calling attention to itself. It enhances the comedic effect of the film without ever interfering with the action or the dialogue. At the other extreme, Nino Rota's scores for *The Godfather* films support the tragedy depicted, but again with transparency and economy; what could easily slip into mere pathos or melodrama remains honest and deeply felt. (Young composers would do well to study these films as examples of how to score comedy and tragedy.)

Another way to determine the overall tone of a film is to examine the main and recurring characters. Just as a psychiatrist's job is to ask questions, so it is with a film composer: How do the main characters progress emotionally through the film? What are the dramatic turning points in their stories? In most dramatic films, the central characters must confront something about their relationships with one another, or their feelings about themselves, and these confrontations change them in some way. A composer must look for these moments for clues to the thematic elements of the score. For example, in Jerry Goldsmith's wonderful main title theme for *Patton,* he hints at both the military and religious aspects of the main character. Trumpet voluntaries in deep echo, repeated in echo delay, express the military aspects; an underlying organ is added as a touch of Patton's religious nature. These two extremely diverse musical elements create an aura of mystery and foreboding. Goldsmith also created distinctive sounds that are repeated and developed at key points later in the film. He saw the film as a total experience, and by hinting at Patton's angels and demons in the main title theme of the film, he sets up a beautiful anticipation to the film's climax, when Patton will realize how the conflict within him has brought him down.

Emotions vary not only in kind, but also in intensity. A touch of anxiety is far different from stark terror, a wry smile is different from a ribald belly laugh, a mild infatuation is different from an obsessive love affair. A perfectly calm scene can be made horrifying by a look in an actor's eyes; a smirk can bring a feeling of scorn and contempt. Music can mirror and reflect all these subtleties in emotional content. As a great actor can bring many subtleties to the emotional complexity of a character, so the composer can reflect these subtleties with music. The composer must watch for and address these underlying emotions. Who can forget the mournful solo trumpet reflecting the loneliness and sadness of Al Pacino's character in *The Godfather?* At the emotional level, the film is about being totally alone in a world without love, and the echoing trumpet was a wonderful choice to reflect this loneliness.

As you explore various emotions musically, it is a good idea to keep a notebook and to sketch some basic thematic ideas as they come up, perhaps even identifying the emotions they express, such as pathos, rage, and loneliness. It is also interesting to try these thematic ideas on various solo instruments to see which instruments best lend themselves to the desired emotion. This sketchpad of brief ideas will ultimately lead to main themes. One is always "panning for emotional gold." In Chapter 17, we will consider some of the specific musical techniques for rendering the basic emotions.

Pace, Tempo, and Rhythm

Let's begin by distinguishing between these closely related terms as they are commonly used in both film and musical jargon. *Pace* is the word for the momentum and flow of an unfolding story. When pace is strong, we are caught up and impelled by the flow of the dramatic action, and time ceases to exist outside the world of the film. Music is the most powerful force to enhance—even provide—such compelling pace. I cannot count the number of times a director has asked me, "Can you help move this scene along?"

Pace is not the same as tempo, although the two are closely related. *Tempo* is the actual speed with which the film moves. A film may have good pace whether its tempo is as slow as that of *The Godfather* or as fast as that of *The Pink Panther.* Good pace means that the story is moving in a strong, unbroken flow whatever its tempo.

The questions I ask myself in these early viewings of the film therefore include, how strong is the overall pace of the film? Are there times when it loses its momentum, and can music help at these times? Can I help to improve the pace and movement it needs? The techniques of enhancing the pace of a scene or of an entire film are ones a composer must learn.

Tempo, apart from pace, deserves its own consideration, and during these first viewings I pay special attention to the tempo of a film and the emotional implications of that tempo. A slow film can be reflective (like *The Last Emperor* or *The English Patient*), or it can have the inexorable drive of destiny unfolding, as in a Greek tragedy (like *The Godfather III* or *In the Bedroom*). A fast film, on the other hand, can have the light quickness of a farce (like *Moulin Rouge* or *A Fish Called Wanda*) or the suddenness of things racing out of control (like Hitchcock's *Vertigo* or most action films). Tempo must be understood in context.

Rhythm is a general term that is used to describe the particular flow of any experience or event that moves through time—not only its speed or tempo, but also the specific pattern of the rise and fall of its energy. This idea can be applied to music, a play, a film, poetry, a sports event, and so on. In music, rhythm usually refers to the particular pattern of stressed and unstressed beats within a measure. Some of these rhythmic patterns are recognizable by tradition, like the ONE-two-three of waltz time or the BOOM-boom-boom-boom of the Native American tom-tom. When some rhythms appear in certain settings and voices, they may have emotional and cultural implications that can be especially important to film composers. For example, the familiar military drums that open the main title theme of *The West Wing* immediately establish the sense of power that is important to that series' subject matter. Rhythm, even without melody and harmony, can provide a powerful musical experience. For this reason, most experts say that it is the most fundamental musical element. It certainly speaks most directly to our emotions and to our overall sense of arousal.

Rhythm in film music is rarely constant. An unchanging rhythm throughout a film would, in most cases, work against the dynamic build that is required for good pace. Rather, the rhythm of the score must reflect—or perhaps counterpoint—the ebb and flow of the dramatic action. Often, we will establish a rhythm in order to then work against it; a change in rhythm can be an effective means of providing pace, placing emphasis, and building tension. One of the most famous examples of such a use of rhythm is John Williams's "Shark Theme" from *Jaws*. The motif starts and stops, then starts again and stops again. This jagged rhythm is far more suspenseful and foreboding than if Williams had set up a steady rhythm from the beginning of the cue. In addition, after this jagged rhythm is firmly established, a flowing baritone horn solo provides a beautiful and suspenseful counterpoint to it.

The starting and stopping quality of the theme from *Jaws*, by the way, demonstrates the power of silence, which is something all young film composers must learn. Film itself is continuous; it runs steadily from start to finish. The purposeful use of pauses and silences in the music provides a counterpoint to the flow of the film and can be a very effective method of adding pace, anticipation, and emphasis. Silence is music too, and it is neither necessary nor desirable to have music throughout a film or a given musical cue.

Yet another way to think about the tempo and rhythm in a particular film is to study the way the actors use them. The great acting teacher Stanislavski taught that "temporhythm" (his word for the underlying tempo of a scene and the variations within it) can, all by itself, awaken an actor's participation in the life of the character. Just so, the temporhythms of the underscore should respect, reflect, and enhance the rhythmic aspects of the actor's performance. As I watch the film, I ask myself, what is the tempo of the dialogue? Are there stage waits? How fast is the cueing between speeches? Are there changes in the tempo of the actors' performances? If so, where do they happen, and what do they signify? All these observations have tremendous implications for the score.

Genre and Style

As Michael Brown explained in Part Two, *style* is not to be confused with *genre*. A genre, such as romantic comedy, western, suspense thriller, or fantasy adventure, is a category of film about which we have certain expectations and that may employ a certain vocabulary of dramatic elements and music. Sergio Leone's "spaghetti westerns" starring Clint Eastwood, for example, had similar structures, characterizations, and values (a lone, mysterious hero overcomes a lot of bad guys, and justice prevails). A musical vocabulary established by tradition exists within each genre; for example, when the spaghetti western moved to Hollywood, Dominic Frontiere's score for *Hang 'Em High* respected the parameters established by Ennio Morricone's Italian originals. Not all films are genre films, of course, and not all genre films conform to the rules of their genre, nor should their music. Just as *Shane* and *Unforgiven* transcended the western genre, so too did their scores (by Victor Young and Lennie Niehaus, respectively) transcend western movie music.

Style, as distinct from genre, is the particular mark of a given artist, the personal way in which he or she has combined form and content to achieve the final product. In this sense, every film has a style, and since movies are primarily a visual medium, it derives mainly from the director. To produce a unified result, everyone who works on the film must recognize, respect, and conform to the style established by the director. This, of course, includes the composer, who might have an individual compositional style, just as an actor might have his or her own way of acting, but composer and actor alike must adapt their approach to provide a result that, although it will remain personal to them, will nevertheless function within the parameters of the style established by the director.

This, however, leaves enormous latitude to the composer. There are an almost infinite number of ways that music can function within the style of a film. A number of years ago, an interesting experiment was performed. Four different and accomplished professional composers were given the same scene from an episode of *Lassie* and asked to score it. There was no communication among them on how to approach the scene. The resulting scores were entirely different from one another. One composer took an atonal and jagged approach; another played the scene with percussion only; another wound up with a continuous, insistent theme; and the fourth chose a more lyrical and romantic approach. And guess what? They *all* worked! True, each gave a different emotional and dramatic tone to the scene, and the director would have undoubtedly preferred one over the others, depending on his intention for the scene. But viewed in the abstract, they all provided an effective underscore to the scene because all four of the composers were skilled in the art of accompaniment. They all knew how to deal with action, emotion, characterization, and pace and how to relate to dialogue and sound effects. There was, in fact, no *one* way to score the scene, no one perfect solution, only a choice to be made within the limits established by the intention of the director.

Developing and Presenting the Concept

Through early viewing of the film, analysis, rumination, and sketching, an overall approach to the score begins to emerge: ideas about tonal quality, the rhythmic and harmonic base, and—most important—the central theme or themes.

The central theme serves as the touchstone for the film, the basis for many variations that appear throughout the film. The overall scores of many films conform roughly to the principles of sonata form, called ABA', or statement, development, and recapitulation. In a movie, the *statement* of the theme is often made in the main title; the cues in subsequent scenes *develop* that theme in variations, changes of key, voicing, and rhythms as the action evolves; finally, a *recapitulation* of the theme (and a return to the tonic key) occurs at the climax of the picture. (A film that focuses on several relationships, such as Woody Allen's *A Midsummer Night's Sex Comedy,* might have three or more coequal themes that coalesce at the end to provide a sense of climax. This would reflect the *linear* form of composition rather than the *sectional* form of the sonata.)

Choosing the main theme is obviously tremendously important, since it will serve as the basis for many of the cues in the picture. Over the years, one of the things I've learned to do before committing myself to a theme is to experiment with it in the more important scenes of the film: the main title theme must not only establish the mood of the film; it must also work in the pivotal scenes of the film itself.

Choosing the *musical palette* for the film is also important. Which solo instruments best convey the desired overall mood? What is the best instrumentation for this film? *Star Wars,* for example, was a film about a fantastic, highly technological future; it might have suggested the use of equally fantastic, technological electronic music. But John Williams chose a traditional live symphony orchestra instead. He told me why: He wanted the music to anchor the audience in something familiar. "That way they could better accept all the 'far out' things on the screen," he said. "A Western in space," he called it, and he wanted the music to be immediately accessible to the ear so that it would not push the picture "over the edge." His overall concept for *Star Wars* therefore harkened back to the opulent symphonic scores of the great westerns and classic adventure movies, such as Dmitri Tiomkin's score for *Rio Bravo* with John Wayne or Erich Korngold's score for *Captain Blood* with Errol Flynn.

Having begun to develop an overall concept, with some ideas about the themes, palette, and rhythm I wish to use, I make a demo CD that presents these ideas to the director and producers. Receiving early approval of a concrete example of my ideas, not merely a verbal description that can be so easily misunderstood, will save a world of hurt later on. I try not to spend more than a day or so producing the demo, as there surely will be suggestions for modification; I find that if I invest too much energy in the demo at this point, I might become protective of it, defensive, and resistant to the changes that will surely be made. Instead, I use the process of making the demo as a heightened form of exploration. I try various things; if I intend to use a solo instrument or small cluster of instruments to carry the theme, I experiment with samples of those instruments. I make brief recordings of rhythmic patterns and play them against a few scenes from the film to see how the pace feels. I'm not going for a finished composition; I'm just exploring. If a given tempo and rhythmic pattern are working, I put them on the sample CD. If the director and producers like what I've done, I can later develop it further. Often, what they really like about a given cue is its tempo and overall tone, and the specifics are of no real consequence.

Spotting and the Music Editor

Once the basic musical approach has been approved and soon after the cut has been locked, a *spotting session* will be held. The director and composer, along with the sound supervisor and the music editor, will sit down in front of a monitor and run a tape of the film, stopping and starting as they discuss each scene, spotting where music will start and where it will end, with the music editor taking copious notes. This is the most important discussion of the entire process.

The first and most important question in each scene is, should there be music here or not? As we have said, it is important to remember the power of silence, that the absence of music can be just as effective as music itself. Often, films are "overspotted," with too much music because directors and editors are afraid that pace and emotion will suffer if every second isn't tracked. They think of silence as a dead spot. This kind of thinking can be detrimental to the end result, for if music does not add something positive to a scene, its pointless presence will ultimately detract; it will call attention to itself and feel gratuitous. The best way to avoid overspotting a film is to work backwards, to first identify the scenes that definitely need music, then go back and carefully evaluate the remaining scenes, asking, why should there be music under this scene, and if so, what are we trying to accomplish with it?

When you have agreed that there should be music under a particular scene, you must also determine its function. Should the music simply add pace? Should it establish mood? Should this music relate to main themes established in the film? Should the music sneak in or start emphatically? How should the music blend with the sound effects? And in the back of his or her mind, the composer is always thinking about the integrity and progression of the total score.

The discussion during the spotting session requires skill from both composer and director on how to verbalize about this nonverbal art. The irony is that the more a director speaks in musical terms, the less useful his or her comments are likely to be to the composer. The best strategy is to keep the conversation centered on emotions and specific dramatic requirements: "He should feel lost here, confused, there is no clear way out" is far more useful than "an oboe solo would be good here."

Once the spotting of each cue has been determined, the music editor prepares a special tape of the show, with markings over the picture showing the beginning and ending of each cue and diagonal lines that move up and down the picture indicating **fades.** The composer uses this tape while composing and again later, while conducting the scoring session.

The music editor is the composer's right-hand man or woman. Different composers use the music editor in different ways. Some have close, ongoing relationships, like that of a picture editor and his or her assistant, with the editor attending to the equipment in the composer's studio and participating in aspects of the compositional process. The music editor might help to create electronic augmentation of the underscore, such as machine tracks of synthesized percussion or strings; later, during the recording session, the music editor will "play" this electronic material as if it were an instrument. Still later, during the final mix, the music editor will play a crucial and active role (more on this later).

CHAPTER

17 Composing

We hire composers around here, not critics.
—Lionel Newman, then Head of Music, 20th Century Fox

What steps are to be taken on the sometimes arduous journey to a finished score? Each film composer, like every kind of artist, has his or her own creative process and approaches the craft in a different way. What follows is what has worked for me.

Getting Started

One of the hardest things to do is simply to start. Soon after arriving in Los Angeles, I landed a job on the music staff at Universal Studios. One of the other writers was an immensely talented composer whose work I admired. He was an intense fellow and locked himself in one of the composing rooms to work on a film. We didn't see him again for two weeks. A few days before the scoring session was scheduled, with the copyists waiting for parts and the orchestra soon to arrive, the studio's music director asked me to go in and see what the heck was going on. I knocked on the door, and after a time, the composer, unshaven and ill-kempt, let me in. I asked, "How are you coming along?" He threw up his hands. I glanced at the music paper on his desk, and to my complete amazement, it was totally blank. Two weeks and *nothing*! "I haven't been able to think of anything I like," he said. Needless to say, it was his last job at Universal. It was a shame; there was nothing wrong with his talent or skill, but he had succumbed to the pressure and anxiety of starting to write.

Writer's block is a real and potentially debilitating condition that can strike any composer at any point in the process, but it can be especially severe when it is time to start and that blank piece of paper looks like the doorway to another dimension that threatens to swallow us whole. All composers experience this to some degree, but the successful ones learn how to deal with it and get on with the job. In my experience, the best strategy is to find the courage and patience to put aside expectations. Expectations create tension, and tension at this stage will impede the free flow of ideas. As simplistic as this might sound, writer's block most often comes from the fear of failing to meet expectations.

I find it best to start small and easy. I sketch a few ideas and not just the first ones that come to mind; I sketch this, I sketch that, and I sketch some more. The more raw material I can collect at this stage, the better. I keep the pressure off, remembering that these early ideas are private; they are simply experiments that might or might not work, possible building blocks I might or might not want to use later. The main thing is that I am underway.

I avoid working at the piano or synthesizer keyboard at this stage and instead do my sketches on music paper. This helps to keep my early melodic ideas simpler and less forced. The piano will come later, when it is time to harmonize and develop things more fully; grappling with the piano in this starting phase seems to invite frustration and the temptation to fall back on something familiar. The process of sketching these initial ideas might take a few days, but they will come. The film is leading me on a musical journey, and I need to take some time at the outset to find the path. Gradually, through trial and error, the way will begin to reveal itself; the journey will gather momentum and begin to carry me along.

Scoring a Scene

Once I have gathered my ideas and found the central thematic material and proper musical palette for the film, it is time to start developing and filling out the ideas, scene by scene, cue by cue. There are a number of specific ways in which music can be designed for a scene.

Let's imagine that I am scoring a scene that is set in a church; Jane has come here, troubled because she is attracted to a mysterious man and is considering being unfaithful to her husband of many years; her husband finds her; she confesses; after a suspenseful moment, he laughs; he was her mysterious lover in disguise, testing her! Outraged, she throws her wedding ring in his face and leaves. One way to approach this scene would be to *play through* it (to have continuous music from start to finish) as an "umbrella" for the underlying emotions. At the spotting session, however, I suggest that this might blur the extreme shifts in emotion that occur in the scene and generalize it so as to reduce suspense. Instead, the director and I agree that there should be music at the top of the scene (cue A) and that the music will stop when Jane confesses (thereby building suspense), then resume as Jane realizes that she has been duped by her husband and throws the ring (cue B).

As I consider the possibilities for these cues, I avoid jumping too soon to obvious choices for a "church scene," such as organ music or Gregorian chant; this would be "scoring the scenery." Instead, I consider other possibilities that will better address the dramatic action of the scene. I ask myself, what is really going on here? The action is one of deception, betrayal, and the tearing asunder of a relationship; this suggests some vivid musical possibilities that might counterpoint and enrich the action. There is also that moment when Jane throws her ring; music can catch such specific actions in very precise ways, often in fractions of seconds, and the very moment the ring falls to the floor might suggest a low minor "hit" as the start of cue B.

I also consider ways in which this scene relates to the whole picture: How are the plot and meaning of the story advanced by this scene? Are there recurring themes in it? Perhaps the film is about the ways in which people betray those they love, and we have seen this happen in other scenes and with other characters. It would be useful, in this case, to establish a theme or leitmotif for betrayal. (A leitmotif, from the German meaning "dominant theme," is a thematic passage associated with a particular character or element of a story; the concept was central to the operas of Wagner). A variation of the "betrayal theme" might make up cue B. (To be a useful leitmotif, a theme should be recognizable in a few notes and not take long to develop. Think of those few notes from the shark theme in *Jaws* or the first measures of *The Pink Panther*.) This kind of interweaving of recurring thematic material will help to create a sense of unity, both dramatically and musically, placing this scene in proper relationship to the whole story and this cue in relationship to the whole score.

In fact, one of the main functions of film music is to help unify the theatrical experience for the audience, guiding them through the journey of the story and helping them know where they are, both structurally and emotionally. Music helps to move us from location to location, helps to define changes in mood, reinforces recurring ideas, and so on, all of which are aimed at unifying the experience. As I work, I avoid the temptation to look at the film only scene by scene, cue by cue; working in this way can make the score choppy and disjointed.

Expressing Emotion

Perhaps the richest source of inspiration for the composer is the emotion of the scene. As we have said, music is deeply involved with emotion, and film music in particular is most effective when addressing emotion. In the church scene, for example, fear, love, and rage are all involved at various points. Let's take a look at some specific compositional techniques that can be used to express these basic emotions.

Fear, anxiety, danger, dread, and unease, all of which heighten suspense, are ever-present screen emotions. Some musical voicings to express fear include low woodwinds (bassoons and bass clarinets), low strings (cellos and basses), French horns in the low register, trombones in straight mutes, and low piano or harp. We might also use percussion, such as soft timpani, ominous cymbal rolls, or a more exotic color such as scraping a rubber ball on a large gong (a horrifying sound). Any one of these sounds will produce a feeling of impending danger. They can be utilized individually or in various collective combinations, although in film scoring, less is more, so orchestral timbres should be clear and uncluttered. I have always been a believer in *transparency* in orchestration; through clarity and economy, the music should not call attention to itself, but rather let us see the scene more clearly *through* it.

Love in its many forms, from passionate lust to gentle romance, is a film staple. How best to express musically some of the subtleties of the feeling of love? First, I have found that more than any other emotion, love requires *melody*. It is no coincidence that love songs loom large in the history of film music, many of them as main themes; many have become musical classics independent of their movies, such as "Laura" by David Raksin, the theme from *The Sandpiper* (which became "The Shadow of Your Smile") by Johnny Mandel, and "Moon River" by Henry Mancini (from *Breakfast at Tiffany's*). The art of good melody writing can be a particular asset to a film composer, albeit an elusive one, and is never more important than in dealing with love.

The proper orchestration of a love theme can range from a solo instrument (flute, violin, piano, harp, oboe, and English horn are particularly beautiful) to a full orchestral "tutti" (Italian for *everybody,* meaning that all the instruments in the orchestra, or in a certain section of the orchestra, play at once). Love themes are most often rendered with lots and lots of strings. Longing is often a component of love, and love themes that express longing are usually in a minor key. However, a love theme will require many variations as it progresses through a score, and one that alternates between major and minor keys offers a greater range of compositional possibilities and emotional power than one that is exclusively in a minor key. This can be accomplished by having an A section in minor and a B section in major. Once again, transparency and simplicity will lead to the most effective results.

Humor on any level deeper than slapstick farce is one of the most elusive qualities for a composer. What is "funny" and what is "serious" is extremely subjective. For a number of years I found myself typecast as a composer for comedies, having written the score for the feature film *Breaking Away* and the scores for a number of sitcoms such as *The Mary Tyler Moore Show.* The secret of my success in comedy was that I didn't try to *make* anything funny, I just let it be funny; that is, I tried to provide a musical atmosphere in which the comedy could happen. A light touch of rhythm might be just enough to provide this atmosphere, with very little accompanying orchestration. I have also found that if something is truly funny on the screen, it is probably better to leave the music out completely and let the comedy stand on its own.

Sustaining Pace

One of the most interesting and challenging aspects of scoring a film is to support the pace of each scene and of the overall film as well. This is a crucial skill for any film composer to master.

Pace can be enhanced by melodic means, especially the orchestral technique we call *movement,* the use of swirling or tumultuous patterns of sound. But more commonly, pace is heightened by rhythmic means and especially by increases in tempo or sometimes by the reverse, a *caesura*—a sudden stopping and silence. Compound rhythms (*polyrhythms*) can also be useful, such as playing one rhythmic ingredient at a pulsating pace against another at a more serene tempo. Repetition can enhance pace, such as a repeated pattern on a harp, piano, or percussion. The most extreme example of musical repetition is an *ostinato,* a short musical phrase that is repeated constantly in the same pitch (appropriately, the word is from the Italian for "stubborn"). Indeed, the repeated use of almost any sound will invariably add pace. The trick is not to overuse the sound so that it becomes annoying.

Through the use of *sampling,* computer technology allows the composer to use even real sounds as part of the score, as a kind of *musique concrete.* For the TNT film *Kingfish,* for example, I sampled a wordless, humming, vocal sound as a leitmotif for one of the main characters. I sampled the voice in a number of keys to make sure that no matter where I inserted it, it would fit into the music being played; in effect, the voice sample became another instrument. The voice, at a low level, was then woven into melodic themes played by live musicians. The effect was somewhat eerie, which is exactly what was required. The creative use of samples is an area of film composition that is in its infancy but holds a lot of promise.

Paradoxically, pace can sometimes be achieved by doing the very opposite of what one might expect. For example, the TNT film *Geronimo* contained a climactic four-minute **montage** filled with gruesome killings and barbarism. The scene came fairly late in the film and was preceded by many battles that I had scored more or less conventionally. This montage, however, was not just another battle; it had special importance in the story and needed to stand out as the moment when things had at last gone too far and it was time for the killing to stop. The director, Roger Young, and I decided to try scoring the montage with a lyrical and poignant *adagio* (a slow and lyrical composition) for strings. This was a tonal palette that was the very opposite in quality from the horrific images of the montage, in a tempo that was the reverse of the frenetic action on the screen. We hoped that by turning the tables in this way, the music might be able to comment on the tragedy depicted on the screen rather than simply accompany it. (This was an idea that was highly developed by the German composer Kurt Weill in his work with the playwright Bertolt Brecht.)

I decided to try an additional technique to set the music for the montage apart, and this was an idea born of technology. I scored the scene preceding the montage with synthesized strings; they sounded real enough, but at a deep level, they lacked "soul." As the montage began, the synthesized strings were transformed into the real strings of our orchestra. This was done by simply lowering the faders on the mixing console that contained the synthesized strings and simultaneously raising the faders on the channels containing the real strings. It was as if the strings had blossomed, as if the warmth of life had been breathed into a barren landscape; that human warmth stood in stark contrast to the inhuman cruelty depicted on the screen. The effect was stunning, and many of the hardened veterans on the mixing stage were deeply moved.

Notice, by the way, that this unorthodox approach was made possible only by the level of trust that had been established between director and composer.

CHAPTER

18 Finishing

They don't want it good, they want it Tuesday.
—Alfred Newman, Composer

The first draft of the score is done. Before it can be performed and recorded, it has to be approved by the director and producers, and they will expect to hear fully fleshed out and programmed demos. These demos are usually made electronically. In some special cases, I have brought a few soloists, sometimes even a vocalist, into my studio and recorded some live elements for the demo. (This is an expense that ideally the producers will agree to add to the budget or to the music package fee.)

At this point, the composer must face a critical choice: How much of the finished score will be synthesized on the computer, and how much will be performed by real, live musicians? Or, as we say, how much machine, how much live? If you are working on a low-budget independent or student film, the choice is easy; you will create the entire show in the machine, with the aid of perhaps one or two soloists, and the whole thing will be recorded and mixed in your home studio. What you hear from the machine is what you get.

In other, more opulent situations, in which the end result is to be performed by a live orchestra, the demo disc might not be an accurate representation of the final product, and this can present problems. What might sound good when played by sampled synthesizer strings might sound crude when played by a real string section. In general, lovely music that demands the nuances and warmth of a live performance often sounds lifeless in the synthesized version, and the cue might be rejected before it can be recorded. It is difficult to convince producers and directors that something that sounds irritating on a demo will sound good later with real instruments; most non-musicians prefer to trust the evidence of their own ears.

I try to work around this problem by programming a demo disk that both sounds good enough to get approval and will also sound good later when recorded with a live orchestra. This means finding sounds that sound good both "synthesized" and "real," and this rules out some sounds. Soft string tremulos, for example, sound wonderful with real strings, but I have yet to find an electronic sample I like, so this is one of the orchestral colors that I avoid. Likewise, some woodwinds don't sound quite right on the computer for the simple reason that machines don't breathe. Over the years, I've written for orchestras of all kinds as well as for the computer, and as good as computers have gotten to be, I still find computer-generated technology to be limited in its musical range.

Approving the Score

As I prepare demo CDs containing actual cues for the show, I begin to present them for approval a few at a time. I try not do too much all at once. Unless the amount of music in the show is minimal, it is too much for anyone, me included, to deal with an entire score all at once, so I normally present only about ten major cues at a time, leaving incidental odds and ends to be cleaned up later.

This can be the most frustrating and exhausting phase of the entire compositional process. Except in very rare circumstances, you can expect a host of sometimes conflicting notes from the director, producers, and executives. Every cue will be thoroughly discussed and perhaps revised, rediscussed, and perhaps revised again; it goes with the territory. Here are a few techniques I have learned along the way that help me through this nerve-wracking time.

First and most important, I try to remain objective and not take comments and criticisms personally. Like any committed professional, I have a lot of ego invested in the music I write, but I try to remember that the comments are not judgments on my talent. In fact, the comments might not even really be about the music. Music is one of the most subjective art forms, and it functions as a sort of Rorschach test; comments about music often reveal more about the person making them than they do about the music itself.

Second, I keep my communication direct; I never deal with assistants or someone who is "translating" the ideas of someone else; the result can be a Tower of Babble. For this reason, I try to present the cues in person, sitting together in a screening room or sound studio. I have usually already given the director and producers demos of the themes, orchestrated according to the musical palette I've chosen, so they have already become accustomed to my musical approach. This gives us a good basis for constructive discussion of the specifics.

Third, I try to keep my reaction to comments balanced. Becoming defensive will never work, but being overly compliant is not the way either. I try to take comments in a collaborative spirit, looking always for opportunities to improve the work but standing up for the things I consider fundamental to the music and to my integrity as an artist. Of course, balance works both ways. A skilled director or producer will try to balance criticism with praise. "I love the first part of the cue, but I have a problem with the end," he or she might say. This kind of comment provides a good basis for further discussion and even on-the-spot experimentation. However, the praise with which criticism is balanced is sometimes a mere smokescreen. It sometimes goes like this: "I love the oboe! That is an oboe, isn't it?" Your response might be, "Actually, it's an English horn, but they are so close most people wouldn't know the difference." "Well," they go on, "whatever it is, I love it, *but—*" Its funny how there always seems to be a "but," and it signals that we have now reached the real objection. They continue, "It feels too slow. Can't you speed it up? Maybe it needs more notes, I don't know, but it's far too slow. The whole cue is too slow. The whole *score* is too slow."

Finally, I try to keep the comments as specific as possible. When a cue is discussed, I try to probe for more specificity in the comments; I ask questions, I listen. What are they really saying? When we get past the confusion caused by words, we often discover that what's bothering them might require a very simple musical fix; it might even be possible to fix it on-the-spot at the synthesizer keyboard. But sometimes the comments are more fundamental, and I have to make a difficult choice: Should I try to fix the existing cue (which might commit me to a whole series of rewrites), or should I just write a whole new cue from scratch? The choice can be made only in each individual instance.

If I believe the criticism is so fundamental that it requires a complete rewrite of the cue, I usually make note of it and suggest that we go on to other cues and come back to the problem cue later. The momentum of the meeting is important, and I don't want to get bogged down arguing about just one cue. It is crucial that everyone understand the cues within their musical context. Sometimes, listening to the rest of the cues can even solve what was thought to be a problem with an earlier cue. The important thing is that everyone hears how the cues relate to each other and not just listen to them individually. If they can feel how the music is working as an integrated whole, their criticisms usually become much more minor and manageable.

There is one terrible situation in which nothing will help. This occurs when the composer is caught in the middle of a power struggle between the director and the producer, when they totally disagree on the music and neither will yield; in such a case, agreeing with one will alienate the other. There is no real way out of this double bind. The best advice is the one given in Shakespeare's *Hamlet:* "To thine own self be true."

Unfortunately, there are some directors, producers, and executives who will never be satisfied. There is one major executive in Hollywood who is infamous for firing the first composer on almost every film he controls, perhaps just to prove that he can. Thankfully, there are many more directors, producers, and executives who are very appreciative of composers and their work. The most extraordinary experience I ever had was when I scored a picture called *Casey's Shadow* for the great director Martin Ritt. I went to the spotting session, and we had no sooner sat down when he said, "Look, I don't know a thing about music . . . but that's why *you're* here, so just do what you think is right." He promptly left the room, leaving me sitting there, dumbfounded and delighted. In all my years in the business, that was the *only* time that has ever happened. By the way, I thought the score turned out extremely well, and he did too.

Working with Sound Effects

One of the most challenging aspects of being a film composer is working with sound effects. How music and sound effects work together is crucial to the total experience the audience will have of the film. This coordination of music and sound effects is made more difficult by the realities of postproduction. The composer and the sound effects editor do not usually work together; they might not even meet until the final mix. Normally, there is one spotting session for music, with no sound effects editor in attendance, and another spotting session for sound effects with no composer in attendance. In these cases, it is wise to ask the director, editor, or sound supervisor about the plans for sound effects, since it is essential to take sound effects into account while composing. There is a traditional contest between music and sound effects at every final mix, and the composer doesn't want the music to come in second.

One of the things that help a composer to deal with sound effects is *register*. If the effects are likely to be in the low register (as in thunder and explosions), the music can often be more effective in a higher register, where it will not conflict with the sound effects, but rather will surround them. Another aspect is the choppiness or staccato quality of the effects (as in intermittent gunfire), when a more legato musical approach will fare better in the final dub, as the two will not fight each other for attention.

In the spirit of "if you can't lick 'em, join 'em," I have sometimes incorporated sound effects in the score as integral musical elements. A few years ago, I scored a film called *The Cutting Edge*. It was about a figure skater and a hockey player who fall in love and eventually have to skate together. Paul Glaser, the director, and I decided to try to have the score utilize some real skating sound effects. To accomplish this, I entered into a collaboration with the sound effects editor. He sent me a menu of real skating sounds, "whooshing," "stopping," and "swishing." We loaded these sounds into my synthesizer, and I treated them as my percussion instruments. As I began composing cues, however, I quickly found that the skating sounds became distracting and lost their impact unless they were used sparingly; I began using them only for emphasis. I needed a richer percussive palette, so I combined the skating sounds with "vocal percussion." These were sampled human breath sounds and noises; percussive sounds such as "cha" seemed particularly good. The combination was starting to sound distinctive; it was setting a style and mood. I added a brisk eighth-note rhythm pattern and a funky Fender bass, and my rhythm section was complete. I was "off the dime." I sent my rough tracks to the sound effects editor so that he could get up to speed with me, and we created some interesting combinations of music and effects that really did work together. This active collaboration between music and effects was, of course, a rare occurrence, but I hope someday I can do more along these lines.

The Scoring Session

Everything discussed so far happens in a matter of weeks—perhaps only two weeks for television films, perhaps four for more ambitious projects such as cable films and six or more for features (although even these can sometimes be rushed; the ability to work quickly is a valuable quality for a composer to develop).

At last, the cues have been approved, and it is time to record the music. This is called the **scoring session.** The paper scores for each musician have been prepared by an orchestrator and a copyist and double-checked by the composer and the music editor. The needed musicians, those highly versatile studio musicians who can sight-read with extraordinary skill and expressiveness (we sometimes call them "pressure cookers") are hired to the composer's specifications by an **orchestra contractor.** The musicians and any special rented instruments are assembled in a special recording studio, also called a *recording stage.* This studio is soundproof and relatively "dead" (lacking in reverberation) to ensure that the recorded sound will be **dry,** lacking any peculiar qualities of its own. This allows it to be given whatever qualities may be desired through electronic manipulation later.

The various sections of the orchestra (strings, woodwinds, brasses, percussion, and so on) are given their own microphones and are separated by baffles so that there is a modicum of separate control over the recording of each section, although the musicians can still hear one another. Soloists or special instruments might be placed in entirely separate booths for complete isolation, with the performer listening to the rest of the orchestra over headphones. This allows the recording engineer, sitting at a mixing console behind a glass wall, to control the balance between the various instrumental elements. With the engineer in the booth, listening to the session over speakers, are the director, the editor, the producer, the sound supervisor, and perhaps an executive or two.

The conductor, who is often the composer, stands before the orchestra watching a monitor or, on large stages, a projected image of the special tape of the show prepared by the music editor (see Figure 18.1). Each cue is recorded as a separate item, played back, and checked by all concerned before moving on to the next. Breaks and overall work time are strictly controlled by the musician's union.

FIGURE 18.1   A Scoring Session. Patrick Williams conducting.

The score is recorded on many tracks, and the music editor then works with the recording engineer to mix these tracks down to produce the tape that will be delivered to the mixing stage (a task that often has to be performed overnight).

The resources that are available for scoring have changed radically over the years. From the late 1930s through the mid-1960s, Hollywood's studio system was in its heyday. Besides a stable of actors, writers, directors, and editors, each studio had a sixty-piece orchestra on staff full-time. The instrumentation was roughly that of a classical symphony orchestra:

20 violins
8 violas
6 cellos
4 basses
3 trumpets
3 trombones
1 tuba
4 French horns
8 woodwinds
1 harp
2 percussion

During these years, most film composers were well versed in orchestrating for the symphony orchestra, providing orchestral colors by setting solo instruments against rich backgrounds. An orchestral vocabulary of film devices became common, such as the "bent" alto saxophone for sex, staccato bassoons for comedy, and low brass and tremolo strings for danger. Exotic and ethnic percussion instruments were often rented for specific scores.

With the collapse of the studio system in the late 1960s, however, the resident orchestras disappeared along with the contract actors and all the rest. As sad as it was, there were benefits from this change. The old orchestral clichés were abandoned. More important, now that musicians were hired ad hoc, composers were free to invent new instrumental combinations for their film scores. Some of the composers in the forefront of this change were Bernard Herrmann, who used eccentric instrumentations such as ten trombones, ten horns, and a tuba; Henry Mancini, who used big band and pop instrumentation; Johnny Mandel, who used jazz instrumentation; Jerry Goldsmith, who began experimenting with mixtures of electronic and acoustic instruments; and Leonard Rosenmann, who used Schoenberg's twelve-tone compositional technique.

In these heady days between the end of the resident orchestras and the advent of synthesizers and computer technology, composers experimented with new ways to use acoustic instruments to do the same old things, the basic functions of film music: to accompany, enhance, embellish, and unify the film. In *Wait Until Dark,* for example, Henry Mancini created suspense by using two pianos tuned a quarter-tone apart, alternately playing the same note. In *Planet of the Apes,* Jerry Goldsmith had the

French horn players reverse their mouthpieces and blow air through the instruments creating a horrifying effect. Most famous of all, Bernard Herrmann had the violinists violently attack their strings with their bows to produce the "screaming" violins in the shower scene of Alfred Hitchcock's *Psycho.*

In today's world, film composers are still searching, running through endless menus of synthesizer sounds, sampling, tweaking, looking for the "magic bullets" that will give their scores an interesting and fresh twist, looking for new ways to do the same old things: accompaniment, enhancement, embellishment, and unification of their films.

Soloists

An interesting way to achieve individuality and to color a score is through the use of solo instruments. Three main factors will provide individuality and color: the quality of the instrument itself, the register in which the instrument is played, and the personal style of the soloist.

Solo instruments can have individual personalities. A solo French horn, for example, can be lovely and extremely haunting, an E-flat contrabass clarinet can be mysterious and scary, and a solo violin can be romantic and passionate. Using uncommon registers of instruments can also add surprising colors. For example, although a bassoon in its normal lower register is often humorous, if played in its high register it can have a seductive and haunting quality. A cello in the high register is a glorious and extremely intense sound. One word of caution: Solo instruments can be extremely effective, but they must be used judiciously or they can quickly wear out their welcome.

Just as the personal quality of an actor must be weighed in casting a role, so the personal style of a soloist must be considered to gain the maximum theatrical impact from the instrument for the particular purpose. In other words, the musical quality of the player must be married with the theatrical purpose of the music. The difference between a solo clarinet played in a New Orleans style and a classical style, for example, is night versus day. A recent example of both musical and theatrical brilliance that was produced by the perfect selection of a soloist was the use of cellist Yo-Yo Ma in *Crouching Tiger, Hidden Dragon.*

Dubbing

The final step in the process of composing for film involves the rerecording or *dubbing* of the music into the film (also called the final mix). Here, as has already been described in Parts One and Two, the dialogue, sound effects, and music are blended to achieve a unified result.

The dubbing stage is a place that is loaded with potential problems for the composer, and the greatest is the problem of relative loudness or *level* of the music. Every decision about the level of the music versus the level of the dialogue, and especially the level of the sound effects, is put under a microscope, discussed, tested, and retested. The lowering of a fader on a console controlling the score can ruin weeks of work and thousands of dollars of expense. Many a film composer has left the dubbing room muttering expletives and asking, "Why did I spend all this time and effort on this music only to see it covered up by sound effects?"

Today's sophisticated recording technology has even made it possible to alter music cues in the dubbing room. Whereas the various tracks recorded at the scoring session were once irretrievably mixed down to the number of tracks needed by theater sound systems, nowadays they can be manipulated on the spot. "How about if we drop the strings from that cue?" is the kind of comment that can strike fear into a composer's heart. Likewise, cues that were spotted in one place may be slid forward or back: "What if that cue started when she opens the door instead of when he sees her?" True, the cue might start perfectly well in its new location, but will its shape be right? Will it end well? Even more terrifying is the next question: "Can't we make that cue a little longer?" The next thing you know, the music editor is sent scurrying off to the Pro Tools machine to tweak the pitch, the tempo, or who knows what. Worse yet, cues might be swapped: "What if we take the ending of reel one and put it here at the beginning of reel five? It's about the same length." True, but will it make musical sense? Will it fit into the musical progression of the score?

When disputes such as these arise, the final decision about level and placement of music cues is normally made by the director, but in truth, there might be political as well as artistic dynamics at work. Some suggestions are essentially trivial, and others are truly injurious. A composer has to learn to pick his or her battles, yielding on trivial matters in order to fight for the serious ones. Only the composer really understands which is which and what the consequences might be, but sadly, our considerations are sometimes dismissed as the paranoia common to our odd breed. As Andre Previn once said, "Everyone knows their job *and* the composer's."

CHAPTER

19

A Career as a Film Composer

The road to professional success as a film composer is never straight. Many of the breaks that come our way depend on luck and coincidence, things that are totally beyond our control. Yet such happy accidents can be invited and encouraged; we can increase our chances. Then, when fortune smiles on us, we must be ready to seize the opportunity and deliver the goods; we must prepare ourselves for success.

Before any of this, however, before one even embarks on a musical career, the would-be composer must ask himself or herself the fundamental question: Do I have the talent?

Natural Ability

Musical ability often shows up early in life. Some children can easily recognize and reproduce differences in pitch, variations in harmony, and basic rhythm patterns. Melody, harmony, and rhythm are the building blocks of all musical expression. If a child is blessed with these abilities, music can follow. Mozart was composing at an age when most of us are learning to read, but even if one was not a child prodigy—as most of us were not—it is through the experience of the basic musical elements that one grows and develops into a musician. The innate talent of the child must be developed, or the gift may be wasted; experience suggests, for instance, that playing an instrument as a child is helpful to later development of musical artistry. The brain must be given the opportunity to absorb melodic curves, rhythmic patterns, and pleasant harmonies. Whether one sings a nursery rhyme as a child or composes the score to a motion picture as an adult, the same components—melody, harmony, and rhythm—come into play.

But the talent itself remains a mystery, given to some, withheld from others. As Robert Jourdain puts it in *Music, the Brain and Ecstasy,*

> What makes a distant oboe's wail beautiful? Why is one chord "happy," another "sad," another "languished"? . . . And how is it that of billions of brains that have known and enjoyed music, only a handful have been able to invent the music of ecstasy?[6]

[6]Jourdain, Robert, *Music, the Brain and Ecstasy: How Music Captures Our Imagination,* William Morrow & Co., 1997, pp. xii and xiii.

Preparing for the Call

"The call" is that magical moment when someone offers you the chance to compose a film score. It is the moment when preparation meets opportunity meets risk. Those of us who have chosen this career measure our lives by these moments. We do all we can to invite them and to be prepared to answer them successfully.

Before the call comes, it is assumed that the composer will have his or her musical tools sharp and at the ready. How much experience in the craft of music is required? What level of mastery of the basics—melody, harmony, and rhythm—is needed? Can one write a clear, simple melody that can be repeated and transmuted as a theme? Can one harmonize a melody in various ways, including enharmonically? Does one understand how the bass works with the melody in basic counterpoint? Can one keep time? Can one tap out polyrhythms? Can one orchestrate with an understanding of the instruments and how they work? If the answer to these and other questions is yes, the composer is ready. If not, the call will go unanswered.

How and when does the call come? The truth is, in most cases, it doesn't. It usually starts as a rumor: "Did you hear that so and so is looking for a composer?" How does a young composer enhance his or her chances of hearing such rumors, of getting on the grapevine? Luckily, Hollywood is a company town and, as such, has all the characteristics of any small town. Gossip, word of mouth, and perception (who's hot this month and who's not) are all part of the Hollywood game. Even successful careers require constant reinvention. To get started as a composer (or to maintain a career, for that matter), networking, cultivating personal relationships, and perseverance are crucial. Just as melody, harmony, and rhythm are the Holy Trinity of music, networking, relationships, and perseverance are the triumvirate of a career in film music.

Gaining Experience

The first step is to gain experience and credits by actually doing some scoring. Winning the opportunity to do actual work can start with networking.

There are a number of levels on which to network. The best places for an aspiring composer to begin are ASCAP (the American Society of Composers, Authors, and Publishers) and BMI (Broadcast Music Incorporated). As composers' performance representatives, ASCAP and BMI serve the composer, protect performance and publishing rights, and collect the royalties due on both. ASCAP and BMI sponsor seminars, workshops, and panel discussions about the business and even award internships and scholarships to young composers. Each of these performance societies has someone who specializes in composer relations; a young composer should meet this person at each organization and then choose to affiliate with one of them. There is competition between the two organizations, which can work to the advantage of the beginning composer. (BMI can be found on the Internet at *www.bmi.com*, and ASCAP can be found at *www.ascap.com* and, even more usefully, at *www.ascapfoundation.org*, its site for scholarships and other useful material for beginning composers.)

A young composer who is seeking work might investigate the SCL (Society of Composers and Lyricists) in Hollywood. It has approximately one thousand members and though it is not technically a guild, in some ways it functions as one. It sponsors seminars, publishes a newsletter, and has a board of governors. What this organization does, it does quite well, and it can be a valuable asset to a young film composer.

For actual work at the entry level, film schools are the first place to go. Young filmmakers are always looking for young composers to score their films. One cannot expect money or even respect, and one cannot be too choosy about the projects offered. "No" is not an adaptive word for an aspiring film composer. With luck, one might score a film that receives some attention or at the least gain experience and meet young filmmakers who are on the way up.

Writing music for the live theater can be another good source of early experience and credits, so one shouldn't overlook the university drama departments, local community theater groups, the small professional theaters, and even the regional theaters. Good early connections can be made here; many film directors and producers have started their careers in live theater.

Another avenue of entry into film composing is to find an established composer who is overcommitted and offer to do some helping. This can come in a variety of forms, from grunt work to computer programming to orchestration to ghostwriting. Some established composers regularly use helpers, especially composers who rely heavily on computers that need programming; this is where computer skills can really pay off. With some luck, a young composer can make a little money by being a helper, but it will be very little. The real reward is the opportunity to learn a tremendous amount about the process of scoring film, and this experience is worth considerable financial sacrifice.

Some busy composers even turn over some compositional chores to an assistant. Like the apprentice of a Renaissance painter, the assistant might have the chance to complete the background by orchestrating according to the composer's musical design; the assistant might even get to execute the master's sketched ideas, whether written down or not. Here again, at least initially, the word "no" should be avoided. A cheerful and collaborative attitude, not to mention programming and orchestrating skills, will go a long way to help ensure success.

The Demo CD

The first step in preparing for an assault on the movie business requires the making of a demonstration compact disc, or *demo CD,* a sampler of work that serves as an audition for prospective employers. To plan a demo CD, it is best to begin by watching a lot of current movies to get a sense of the kind of film scoring that is prevalent in today's films. When one sees a film with a good score, analyze what was effective about it and what musical resources were used. These observations are useful in preparing one's own demo CD.

How does one actually make the disc? One of the requirements of an aspiring movie composer is computer literacy, at least in the use of the various programs that are used to create music. Armed with this skill, one can find or rent a computer studio and a library of samples (samples are snippets of recordings of real instruments that can be manipulated and combined with others to produce the sound of whatever instrumentation is desired). Using these resources, one can compose sample cues as if composing for an actual film.

The demo CD should contain, at the minimum, several pieces that demonstrate the ability to handle different dramatic moods, such as suspense, humor, sadness, and longing. The examples should not be much longer than two minutes each, and even less; actual film cues are rarely longer than two minutes, and the people who listen to demo CDs are busy and quick to press the fast-forward button. Arrange the sample pieces in a pleasing way, as if programming an album; open with a real "grabber" and then alternate pieces with different moods and tempos and a variety of instrumental sounds, perhaps including a very few examples with an ethnic or regional flavor.

A good all-purpose demo CD must be accompanied by an attractive, truthful resume. One should not be shy about listing student work and the training received in school. Armed with the demo CD and the resume, the fledgling composer is ready to approach prospective employers and/or **agents.**

Agents

Getting an agent is certainly helpful, and while not absolutely necessary at the outset, it is something that every composer will eventually want to do. For most young composers, obtaining an agent is a daunting task, and they confront the same Catch-22 that perplexes all beginning actors, writers, and directors: How do you get an agent without credits, and how do you get credits without an agent?

One starts by obtaining a list of active agents from either ASCAP or BMI. Although ASCAP and BMI cannot recommend a particular agent, the lists will at least help to provide an overview of the professional music community. More important than the list of agents itself is the list of clients of each agent; by examining the client lists, one can identify those agents who handle the kind of composer one aspires to be, and this will greatly narrow the search.

Trying to get an initial meeting with an agent is often tricky. Mailing off the demo CD and resume without personal contact is probably the least effective strategy. It is better to deliver the materials in person, request a meeting, and then follow up with a phone call. Most effective, however, are personal references and recommendations. These could come from a friend in the industry, from another composer who is represented by the target agent, or from a contact at BMI or ASCAP.

Before meeting an agent for the first time, some homework needs to be done. Young composers needs to be clear about the kinds of projects they are looking for and the type of scores they feel most qualified to write. The more concrete one can be about what one wants and what one has to offer, the better are the chances of success.

Once the initial meeting has been held, it is wise to follow up with a letter and a phone call to get the agent's reaction to the demo CD, asking for specific comments. Does the sampler make an effective presentation? If not, what's missing? A good demo is a good start, so an agent's informed reaction to the CD is valuable, even if he or she doesn't end up being one's agent.

Getting an agent does *not* mean that the composer can just turn the problem of finding work over to the agent. The only wise course is to hustle just as if there were no agent at all. In truth, until a career is well established, the forte of most agents is not so much getting jobs as making deals once the jobs have been gotten. Getting the job will still be mainly the young composer's responsibility. Again, that is where the big three come in: networking, relationships, and perseverance.

Payday

When considering a career as a film composer, one must understand some basic financial realities. The picture is not altogether rosy. More often than not, a composer will be under three kinds of pressure: financial, time, and political.

We movie composers must accept the reality of meager budgets and fees, looming deadlines, and, often, demanding employers. To make matters worse, unlike actors, directors, and writers, composers have no guild or union with bargaining leverage, no negotiated Minimum Business Agreement, no standards for minimum wage, and no guidelines for punitive actions when agreements are violated. How much we are paid to score a film, the amount of time we will have to do it, and the conditions under which we will work are totally open to negotiation, so we must depend on our agents to make the best deal possible on a case-by-case basis.

Nor is scoring films a risk-free activity; there are some situations in which a composer can actually lose money on a job. It has become the norm in network and cable television for the music to be contracted as a **music package.** A music package is an arrangement whereby the composer is responsible for delivering the finished score to the final mix, ready for use; the composer is liable for *all* costs of the composing *and* production of that music. Those costs include any computer programming, orchestrating and copying, studio charges, instrument rentals, musicians' salaries and benefits, and agency commission. (In the case of a package, the agent's commission is 10 percent of the composer's **net** profit or 8 percent of the total package fee, whichever is greater.)

Packaging fees for two-hour television movies, for example, might range from as little as $20,000 to as much as $60,000; the current average is about $35,000. After all the costs have been deducted, there is precious little left to repay the composer's talent and effort, and if there are cost overruns in the process of recording the music, the composer must absorb them. Is it any wonder that more and more television scores consist mostly of machine music rather than acoustic performances by live musicians?

In theatrical features, for which music budgets are normally much larger than in television or cable films, the packaging concept is much less common. Here, a composer is paid a creative fee for his or her services, and the other costs associated with actually producing the music are covered by the production budget. Music budgets for feature films tend to run about 1 to 2 percent of the overall film budget, so a $30 million film will have a total music budget of as much as $300,000. The portion of this that goes to the composer is, like everything else, negotiable on an individual basis.

With few exceptions, then, film composers don't get rich, the films we work on are sometimes not the best, and the conditions under which we work can be trying and limiting. Clearly, we do it for much more than the money. Jerry Goldsmith spoke for all serious film composers when he said,

> Motion pictures enable us to experiment, if we are ambitious and daring enough. Don't forget, I can write thirty minutes of music and the day after I'm done I can record it with up to eighty or a hundred of the best musicians in the world, while a man can write symphony after symphony and during his lifetime never hear a note of it played.[7]

[7]Ibid, p. 146.

APPENDIX

A Typical Production Chart of Accounts

Above the Line

Acct#	Heading	Description
1000	Story & Screenplay	
1001		Story Rights
1003		Freelance Writers
1004		Rewrite
1005		Polish

1100	Producer & Supervision	
1101		Executive Producer
1102		Supervising Producer
1103		Producer
1104		CoProducer
1106		Associate Producer
1110		Production Consultant
1112		Technical Consultant(s)
1123		Travel Expense
1124		Living Expense
1125		Box Rentals
1200	Direction	
1201		Director
1207		Director's Assistant
1220		Director Entertainment

1300	Cast	
1301		Lead Cast & Hosts
1302		Supporting Cast
1303		Announcer: On-Camera
1305		Narrator
1307		Specialty Acts
1308		Singers
1309		Dancers
1312		ADR/Looping Allowance
1315		Casting Director
1316		Choreographer
1318		Dialogue Coach
1319		Teacher/Welfare Worker
1340		Teleprompter Rental
1350		Wardrobe Allowance

1400	Music-Production	
1401		Music Director
1403		Librarian

1405		Composing/Arranging
1407		Conductor
1409		Principal Musicians
1415		Purchases
1416		Rentals
1435		Cartage
1450		Music Clearance
1455		Sync./Master Licenses

	Below The Line	

2485		Misc. Expense

2700	Camera/Film	
2701		Director of Photography
2702		Camera Operator
2703		1st Assistant Cameraman
2704		2nd Assistant Cameraman
2715		Purchases/Expendables
2717		Camera Rentals/Accessories
2720		Stillman
2721		Stillman Supplies/Rentals
2725		Box Rentals

3200	Sound	
3201		Sound Mixer
3202		Boomman/Boom Operator(s)
3203		Assistant/Utility Sound
3205		ATR Operator
3206		Sound EFX/Playback Mixer
3207		PA Mixer
3209		Audience Reaction Mixer
3210		RF Technician
3212		Maintenance Engineer
3215		Purchases/Expendables
3217		Sound Rentals
3218		PA Equipment
3219		RF Microphone Package
3220		Walkie-Talkie Rentals
3225		Box Rentals
3300	Special Effects	
3301		Special Effects Man

3302		Additional EFX Labor
3303		SFX Manufacturing
3315		Purchases
3317		SFX Rentals
3325		Box Rentals
3330		Loss & Damage
3385		Misc. Expense
3399		Fringe

3800	2nd Unit	
3801		2nd Unit Director
3802		Production Staff Labor
3803		Set Dressing Labor
3804		Props Labor
3805		Camera Labor
3806		Grip Labor
3807		Electric Labor
3808		Sound Labor
3809		Special Effects Labor
3810		Wardrobe Labor
3811		Hair & Makeup Labor
3812		Transportation Labor
3813		Purchases
1817		Rentals
3885		Misc. Expense
3899		Fringe

3900	Film & Lab	
3901		Negative Raw Stock
3903		Video Stock
3905		Print/Transfer Dailies
3907		DailiesTape Stock
3908		Develop Dailies
3910		Transfer Reprints
3915		Dailies Cassettes
3920		Audio Stock
4900	BTL P/R Taxes & Fringe	
4999		BTL P/R Taxes & Fringe
5000	Editorial Labor	
5001		Post Supervisor
5002		Post Coordinator
5005		Post Assistant
5010		Editorial Supervisor
5011		Editor: Picture

5012		Editor: Assistant
5013		Editor: Apprentice
5015		Editor: Sound
5016		Editor: Music
5020		Editor: Promotion
5099		Fringe

5100	Equipment	
5014		Supplies
5015		Purchases
5017		Rentals
5020		Craft Service
5085		Misc. Expense
5200	"Screening, Storage, Shipping"	
5215		Purchase
5217		Rental
5220		Messengers
5221		Shipping
5222		Customs Fees
5300	Stock Footage	
5301		Research
5315		Materials
5317		License
5320		Amort
5325		Contract Production
5400	"Titles, Credits, Promos"	
5401		Research
5402		Concept
5403		Artwork
5405		Production
5406		Stock
5407		Lab & Transfer
5408		Integration
5410		Promos
5411		Credits
5425		Contract Vendor
5485		Misc. Expense

5500	"Visual Effects, Opticals, Inserts"	
5501		Research
5502		Elements & Artwork
5505		Production
5506		Stock

5507		Lab
5510		Computer Compositing
5511		Film Compositing
5525		Contract Vendor
5585		Misc. Expense
5600	Sound	
5601		Research
5603		Sound Supervision
5605		ADR
5606		Laugh Tracks
5607		Dialogue Editing
5608		Sound Effects
5609		Sound Editing
5612		PreMix/Mixing
5615		Audio Stock
5616		Videocassettes
5625		Contract Vendor

5700	Music	
5701		Research
5702		Supervision
5703		Composer
5704		Musicians
5712		License
5715		Purchase
5717		Rental
5720		Arranging
5721		Scoring
5722		Mixing
5723		Audio Stock
5724		Video Stock
5725		Contract Vendor
5785		Misc. Expense
5800	Film Finishing	
5802		Reprints
5803		Reversals
5805		Negative Cutting
5806		1st Trial
5808		Release Printing
5809		Reduction Printing
5812		Processing
5813		Lab Overtime
5885		Misc. Expense

5900	Video Finishing	
5902		Transfers
5904		Stock: Mastering
5905		Stock: Editing
5906		Stock: Viewing
5910		OnLine Assembly (Mastering)
5915		Color Correction
5985		Misc. Expense
6000	Delivery & Distribution	
6002		As Broadcast Scripts
6005		Formatting
6006		Integration
6008		Film Prints
6010		Video Duplicate Masters
6012		Video Viewing Cassettes
6013		Reversioning
6015		Library Masters
6085		Misc. Expense
6900	Post P/R Taxes & Fringe	
6999		Post P/R Taxes & Fringe

A GLOSSARY OF TERMS FOR FILM AND TELEVISION POSTPRODUCTION

Most of the following terms are marked in boldface the first time they appear in the text. However, in order to provide a more comprehensive glossary, some terms not used in the text have been included.

A and B rolls: The cut negative ready for printing, with each shot alternating between two rolls so that they marry seamlessly into a single composite print. See also *B roll.*

A negative: The shots chosen on the set by the director for possible use, also called "circled takes." See also *B negative.*

Above-the-line: The fee-based costs listed in the topmost section of a film budget, established by negotiation, such as story and writer costs, actor salaries, director costs, and so on. These are distinguished from the weekly costs set by unions and customary rates for craftspeople and rentals, which are *below-the-line.*

Accountant: The person in charge of keeping the extensive books of a film company; issuing the hot cost and weekly cost reports; and handling all payments, salaries, and so on.

Action: What happens in a scene; also, the script element that describes what happens; also, what the director calls to start a shot.

ADR: Automatic Dialogue Replacement, also called "looping," a process in which a loop of film or video is created so that a performer can substitute new dialogue for an existing line while watching the footage.

Agent: A talent representative who submits clients for work and makes their deals, franchised by the appropriate union. Receives a straight commission of 10 percent as the only pay for services.

Analog: The encoding of a signal through the use of analogous voltages representing signal characteristics.

Anamorphic: A type of lens that compresses a wide view so it will fit on a frame of 35mm film, or conversely uncompresses it for projection.

Angle: The position and view of the camera.

Answer print: The approved print reflecting the final timing.

Artifact: An anomaly in a digitally created picture, usually caused by an electronic malfunction.

Aspect ratio: The proportions of the screen on which the show will be projected. Television is the narrowest; feature films are much wider.

Audio time code: The reference numbers on dailies that are generated from the production sound tapes.

Audio: The sound portion of a show.

Avid: The most commonly used computer-driven editing system.

B camera: To save time, two cameras sometimes cover a scene simultaneously, the second being called the B camera.

B negative: Film that was shot but rejected by the director.

B roll: One of the two rolls of cut negative from which a film is printed; also, the video copy of original footage and data usually made to assist in creating a special effect; also, noninterview video footage shot during production by a visiting crew for use in the Electronic Press Kit.

Background: The image over which other images are keyed or matted; also, the people and things that complete the visual environment of a shot, including extras, animals, and vehicles.

Bars: A reference signal recorded on the beginning of a videotape so that the tape can be realigned for subsequent playback.

Baud: Unit for measuring the rate of digital data transmission.

Below-the-line: See *above-the-line.*

Big close-up: The closest shot, face only, also called an "extreme close-up (ECU)."

Bins: In film, containers for hanging strips of film during editing; also, electronic storage areas either on tape, on computer disks, or in an Avid editing system for storing images.

Blow-up: To enlarge the image in the frame by rephotographing it as an optical element.

Breakdown: The script broken down by scene to determine the needs of location, talent, and so on, in order to estimate costs.

Bridging shot: A shot used to cover an edit. See also *cutaway*.

Broadcast quality: The technical specifications of a signal necessary for broadcasting. These extensive specifications define the parameters necessary to legally broadcast pictures and sounds.

Burn-in: Describes the process of adding titles in film or such things as titles and visible data onto videotape.

Card: A typographical display carrying information, such as a credit for one or more persons (single or shared cards), the time and location of the scene, and so on.

CD: A compact disc, a form of distribution, usually for music.

CGI: Computer-generated imagery.

Character generator: A computer or microprocessor for generating letters and symbols electronically.

Chroma key: A process that uses color to determine the specific areas that will be cut out of background in an optical or effect.

Clapper board: The board or slate that is photographed at the start of each take to identify the shot and to establish sound synchronization by the clapping of a stick or, nowadays, a digital display.

Click track: When music is supposed to be playing in a scene, the sound mixer might provide the sound of clicking that establishes the tempo so that the actors can dance or react appropriately. This permits the dialogue to be recorded separately from the music for editing.

Clip: A short segment of a program.

Close shot: A medium close-up, from the chest up.

Close-up: Generally a shot of a person from the shoulders or neck up. Also see *big close-up*.

Color Correction: Changing color shadings in a picture.

Complementary shots: Shots that are the same size but from different angles, designed so that the editor may cut from one to the other freely.

Component: A technical method of recording a color picture that separates the luminance signal from the chroma.

Composite: The encoding of complete video information into one signal.

Composite print: The print that is produced when the A and B rolls or other elements are combined into a single print.

Compositing: The process of combining numerous visual elements in a shot. Special effects generally use this process extensively.

Compression: To proportionally reduce the information in a signal in an ordered manner to allow for subsequent expansion later.

Conforming: Recreating the Edit Decision List (EDL) in either broadcast video or negative film.

Contingency: An allowance in the budget for unforeseen costs, usually 10 percent of the total.

Continuity: The smooth flow of shots and scenes with no disruptions by incorrect details. The script supervisor has the main responsibility for this during shooting, and it is later a major concern of the editor.

Control track: An electronic signal recorded at the beginning of each field of an electronic frame controlling the playback characteristics of the field. It is the electronic equivalent of film's sprocket holes.

Cost report: Issued weekly; shows how much has been spent for each line of the budget and estimates how much remains to be spent for completion.

Coverage: The closer shots taken in a scene to be inserted into the master.

Credits: The main creative credits appear in the main title sequence; the technical credits appear in the end credits. The very first credits are usually the company credits for the financing entities.

CU: Abbreviation for *close-up.*

Cut: (*v.*) To edit, to stop the camera; also (*n.*) a version of the show as edited. The sequence of cuts is usually editor's cut, director's cut, producer's cut, and final cut; also, a relatively abrupt change from one shot to another, as distinguished from a more gradual dissolve. There are several kinds of cuts, such as smash cuts and soft cuts; also, what the director calls to stop a take.

Cutaway: A cut to parallel action in a scene; also, material inserted in a scene to establish mood or place or to cover an awkward edit. See also *bridging shot.*

D&E: Dialogue and Effects, a version of the finished show containing only dialogue and effects but no music. Used for producing trailers and other promotional material that has its own music.

Dailies: The material that is shot on the set and sent to the editing room. In the old film days, these were exposed at a single setting and called one-light dailies; they were also called rushes. Nowadays, film dailies are delivered on videotape or in digital form. Material that is shot in digital (except for HD) is ready for editing immediately.

DAT: Digital audio tape, a cassette format containing stereo sound and sometimes time code.

dB or Decibel: A unit of measurement for sound levels.

Degauss: To demagnetize (erase) all recorded material on a magnetic tape.

Delivery: The final delivery of the film to the financing entity with all the necessary accompanying material listed in the delivery requirements.

Demographic: The age, gender, and/or economic class of a potential audience.

Depth of field: The narrow range in which the camera's subject is in perfect focus.

DGA: The Directors Guild of America.

Dialogue predub: To ready the dialogue for the final mix so as to save time on the dubbing stage.

Digital: A signal encoded in 1s and 0s (binary code) rather than by modulation.

Digitization: The rendering of sound or picture into digital form, as when the dailies are fed into the editing machine.

Dissolve: One of the ways of going from one cut to another. A lap dissolve overlaps one image with another. Dissolves may be fast, medium, or slow. One may also dissolve (*fade*) to black or white.

Double-system: When synchronized sound and picture are recorded or played back separately.

DP: Director of photography; sometimes called the cinematographer; works with the director and is responsible for the "look" of the show, including lighting and camera placement.

Drop frame time code: Time code accurate to clock time to +/– two frames because it drops two frame numbers every minute except the tenth and every hour except the tenth. See also *Non-drop frame time code.*

Dropout: Physically missing information on videotape due to lace of magnetic oxide on the recording medium.

Dry: A recording that is made with no reverberation.

Dub: From "double," to rerecord, as in "to dub his voice." The final mix is often called the dub and is done on a dubbing stage; also, a copy of a tape.

Dubbing stage: Where final mixes are done; a room with a mixing console facing a projection screen.

DV cam: A video camera with higher resolution than VHS, such as Beta or Beta SP, but less resolution than HDTV. Increasingly used for low-budget film production.

DVD: Digital video disc, a distribution medium that encodes much more information than a CD can.

Dynamic range: The range between the softest and loudest sound levels possible without distortion.

ECU: Extreme close-up: See *big close-up.*

Editing: The process of compiling images and sounds into a cohesive program.

Editor: The person who assembles or "cuts" the film together to achieve pace, flow, and good storytelling; there are also sound editors, music editors, story editors, and assistant editors.

Editor's cut: A refined version of the first assembly created by the editor and shown only to the director.

EDL or Edit Decision List: A computer generated or handwritten list of the edits performed during an edit session or in an entire show.

Effect: Any transition other than a cut.

Effects: Sound effects or visual effects, sometimes written as *FX*.

Enhancing: Electronically adjusting the quality and sharpness of a video image.

EPK: The Electronic Press Kit, a video containing interviews and B-roll for use by the press.

EQ or Equalization: Adjusting various frequency ranges of an electronic signal.

Establishing shot: A shot of a location, usually wide, that tells the audience where the action is happening.

Eye-line: The placement of the actor's eyes as he or she looks at someone off-camera.

Fade: A dissolve to or from black or white; also, in audio, the raising or lowering of audio levels.

Favor: When the camera angle throws more emphasis to one character over another.

Feedback: Disturbing sound created by the output of an electronic signal being fed back to the input of the same signal.

Field: Each frame of interlaced video is separated into two fields, each containing 262.5 analog lines.

Final cut: The locked form of the film's visual content; also, control over the final form of the film, rarely granted by a studio to a director.

Final delivery: See *Delivery*.

Final mix: When the sound elements of the show (dialogue, sound effects, and music) are combined and balanced to produce the final sound track. See also *dub*.

First assembly: The first time a show is put together, shown only to the director, also called a *rough cut*.

Flatbed: A film editing machine on which film is cut manually. One common type was the Steenbeck.

Flex file: The telecine transfer log (TTL) that carries the various reference numbers (audio and video time codes and film key code) that enable the editor to access specific takes.

Flipping the negative: Reversing the negative in a particular shot horizontally, usually to match screen direction in adjoining shots. In the Avid system, this is called "flopping," while "flipping" refers to turning the negative upside-down.

Focus group: A representative audience that is brought in to watch a preview of a film and give reactions to it.

Foley: The creation of sound effects synchronized to picture, such as footsteps or glass clinks.

Foreground: The portion of a key signal that appears over another picture.

Frame: One image on a strip of film; also, in video, one (progressive) or two (interlaced) fields of video information comprising 29.97 seconds of real time.

Frame rate: The speed with which film or video frames run.

Freeze-frame: When a singe frame is frozen by being printed over and over; also, the executive producer's credit in some television shows that appears at the end of the story.

FX: See *effects*.

Generation: A count of the level of copies or dubs made of an image, as in "third generation"; especially critical in film and analog videotape.

Glitch: An anomaly in a video or audio signal, caused by an electronic malfunction called a *gremlin*.

Green screen: A method for photographing actors in front of a green or blue background and then superimposing their images over a different background.

Guarantee: The minimum amount that will be paid; also, a letter promising to do something, such as distributing a picture.

Hard disk: A rigid disk, coated with magnetic oxide, for storage and fast retrieval of computer data.

HDTV: High-definition television, a wide-screen format with improved resolution.

Headroom: The area above a person's head in the camera framing.

Held take: A shot that is put on hold by the director for possible consideration.

Hot cost report: A daily report that highlights any unusual expenditures or savings.

Hue: The shade of a particular color.

IATSE: International Alliance of Theatrical Stage Employees, Moving Picture Technicians, Arts and Allied Crafts, the main crafts union, called simply the "IA."

IN: The internegative printed from the interpositive and used for subsequent printing to protect the original negative from the rigors of printing.

In one: Shooting an entire scene in a continuous shot.

Indie: An independently financed film.

Insert: (*n.*) A piece of film that is shot to be inserted into the master, often a POV or establishing shot; also (*v.*), to put a shot between two other shots.

Interlaced video: In ordinary television, only the even numbered lines of the frame are broadcast at one time, followed a thirtieth of a second later by the odd numbered lines. The eye sees these images as one interlaced picture. See also *Progressive video.*

Internegative: See *IN.*

IP: The interpositive printed from the cut negative, used to print the internegatives.

Jump cut: A cut to a similar shot causing objects in the frame to seem to jump.

Kinescope: A crude film recording of a video signal.

Lap dissolve: See *Dissolve.*

Layback: To assemble the various elements of a mix into the final product.

Layering: The building of effects one layer at a time.

Lined script: The script prepared by the script supervisor with all its notations.

Lock: The completion of picture editing; also, the interlock of multiple reels.

Locking the cut: The point after which no further changes in the visual aspects of the show will be made.

Long form: Full-length television movies or films.

Long shot: A distant or wide camera position.

Look: The appearance of the show.

Looping: See *ADR* and *walla.*

Loop group: See *Walla.*

Luminance: The white value of a video signal.

M&E: Music & Effects, a version of the finished show with music and effects only, allowing the insertion of foreign dialogue.

Made-for-cable: A movie made for broadcast by a cable network such as HBO, usually more costly and more adventurous than a network movie-of-the-week.

Main title sequence: The opening credits of a film.

Master log: The record of negative, workprint, videotape, editorial, and audio information for a particular project.

Master shot: The most inclusive view of a scene, usually shot first.

Match: When one thing can be cut to another without disruption.

Matte: A colorized key; also, a high contrast image used to cut a hole in a shot; also, a painted scene that is placed in front of the lens or inserted by composite printing to replace or extend some of the photographed scene, thereby saving construction costs or creating vistas that would otherwise be impossible.

Medium shot: A shot generally from the waist up.

Miniseries: A four- or six-hour movie broadcast on two or three separate nights.

Mix: See *Final mix.*

Mixer: A device to combine various audio sources; also, the name of the person who operates such a device.

Mixing: The process of gathering and combining audio elements into a cohesive whole.

Moiré: A rippling pattern in a video picture produced by harmonic distortion of the signal.

Montage: A series of images, usually without dialogue, that form a single sequence, usually to music, to convey a theme or concept; also, the way adjoining images can produce unique meanings.

Morphing: To smoothly transform an image, such as a face, beginning at one point and ending at another, with the computer providing the intervening material.

MOS: Shot silently, "mit out sound."

Motion capture: A technique whereby the movement of an actor wearing markers read by lasers is captured and translated into computer reference points. The resulting motion can then be assigned to any computer-generated figure.

Movieola: An old-fashioned manual editing machine.

MOW: Movie-of-the-week, or made-for-television movie.

Music package: When a composer is paid a lump sum to compose, record, and deliver the music ready to mix.

NAB: National Association of Broadcasters.

Negative cutter: In film work, the person who cuts the original negative according to the final instructions printed out by the editing machine or copied from the frame numbers on a film workprint.

Negative cutting: In film work, preparing the locked cut for printing by splicing the original negatives into A and B rolls.

Negative pickup: When a partially or completely finished film is sold for completion or enhancement and eventual distribution.

Net: What is left after all costs have been deducted from the gross receipts; a very rare commodity.

Non-drop frame time code: Time code calculated at 30 frames per second. Because television runs at 29.97 frames per second, an error in timing builds up. Drop frame time code corrects this problem.

Nonlinear editing: Editing using a computer-driven system so that the editor can move anywhere within the show at any time.

NTSC: National Television Standards Committee, the standard for color television in the United States, Canada, Mexico, and Japan. This system has 525 lines scanned at approximately 30 frames per second.

Offline edit: Editing that is not meant for final release or broadcast.

Online edit: Editing that produces a final product or broadcast-quality tape.

Optical: When film must be rephotographed to superimpose material, to create a dissolve, to blow up the image, or for some other reason, it is sent to an optical house. The rephotographed film is then inserted into the final negative and is called an optical.

Optical house: The special laboratory where titles, dissolves, and other manipulations of film can be done by placing it in an optical printer.

Optical printer: A machine that prints one frame of film at a time and allows for other elements to be added, or for the picture to be manipulated in various ways.

Optical sound track: The results of the final mix are transferred to a visual form and printed in the margin of a release print. This was how all film sound was recorded on the set before the use of audiotape.

Orchestra contractor: The person who hires the musicians.

PAL: Phase alternate line, the European television format, with 625 lines scanned at 25 frames per second.

Pan: A shot created by swiveling a camera horizontally.

PGA: The Producers Guild of America.

Pickup: Additional footage shot to assist the editor in assembling a scene.

Pixel: A tiny spot on the grid of a digital video picture; thousands of these tiny spots of color are blended together by the eye to produce the finished picture.

Plate: The image projected on an RP screen. See also *RP*.

Postproduction supervisor: The person who guides the film through the postproduction process; in television, sometimes called the associate producer or coproducer.

POV: A shot from someone's point of view.

Practical effects: Effects that are created by mechanical means and simply photographed; these effects are said to be created "in the camera."

Predub: Partial mix of audio elements to simplify the final mix.

Prelay: Sound material prepared in advance for the final mix; also, transferring and editing the audio portion of a production onto a multitrack tape.

Preview: A private showing of a film at an early stage of completion to get feedback on it.

Print: One version of the edited film. There are trial prints leading to an answer print.

Process: Shooting so as to create an effect, such as being in traffic or flying, often using rear projection. "Poor man's process" is the same using lighting or other effects instead of rear projection.

Process stage: A special long narrow soundstage built to accommodate a rear projection setup. See also *RP*.

Producer: The person who guides a film through all phases of its creation. There are various kinds of producing credits, such as executive producer, line producer, associate producer, and coproducer.

Producer's cut: A version of a show reflecting the producer's notes on the director's cut, made before the show is delivered to a network or studio.

Production track: The sound that is recorded when the show was shot.

Progressive video: Computer monitors and high-quality 24pHDTV scan all the lines in the frame in sequence, rather than the odd/even broadcast of lines in interlaced video. See also *Interlaced video*.

Rack focus: To change focus from one subject to another during a shot.

Rainbow script: The shooting script with all its changed colored pages in place.

Release prints: The prints that are sent to theaters.

Reshoot: To redo a portion of a film after wrap.

Resolution: The amount of detail in an image.

Reverb: An electronic audio effect resembling an echo.

Room tone: The natural sounds of a given environment; used to create background fill during a mix.

Rough cut: See *first assembly*.

RP or Rear Projection: By placing a translucent projection screen behind the action, an image (plate) can be projected on it and will appear as the background for the action.

Rushes: What film dailies used to be called because of the speed with which they were processed.

Safe action area: The area that will safely reproduce on most televisions.

Safe title area: The area that will produce legible titles on most televisions.

Saturation: The amount or intensity of color.

Scoring session: The recording of the film's music.

Script supervisor: The person who is in charge of continuity during the shoot. He or she prepares a lined script showing the duration and nature of each shot, with notes, that is invaluable to the editor.

SECAM: Sequential color with memory, the broadcast standard in France, Russia, and Eastern Europe.

Second camera: See *B camera*.

Second unit: A small unit that works separately from the main company to shoot certain material.

Shooting ratio: The amount of film a director uses up to produce a usable result.

Shot: One piece of film.

Shot selection: The editor's choice from among the various takes to produce the best final result.

Shot size: The framing, as in close-up, medium shot, long shot, etc.

Signal to noise: The ratio of unwanted noise present in an analog signal.

Slate: (v.) To identify a shot. This is done for the camera by the clapper board and verbally by the sound mixer on the production tape. (n.) The audio and video identification of the take of a particular shot.

Slow motion: The effect of slowing down a shot; may be achieved either by increasing the frame rate of the recording or by repeating frames of the recorded image.

Smash cut: A jarring, abrupt cut.

SMPTE: Society of Motion Picture and Television Engineers, a group dedicated to standardization of the broadcast industry.

Soft focus: A shot that is not in sharp focus.

Soft cut: A four- or six-frame dissolve.

Sound mixer: The production sound mixer; also, sound mixers who do the rerecording of the show with sound effects and music in the final mix.

Soundtrack: The sound portion of a film. This is usually printed on the edge of the film and read optically, hence an "optical sound track," or may be carried on an electronic medium in dual-system projection.

Sounds-like: Music written by the composer to imitate source music, thereby avoiding the need to purchase music rights for authentic material.

Source music: Music coming from a radio, jukebox, band, or other "live" source within a scene.

Splice: The physical cut on a piece of film or video.

Split edit: An edit in which the picture and sound start at different moments.

Spotting: Locating where the sound effects and music will go in the locked cut.

Sprocket holes: The holes on the sides of film that allow it to be physically moved in cameras, projectors, and telecines.

Stems: The results of the final mix are recorded as three separate synchronized stems, one each for dialogue, effects, and music, permitting various forms of the picture to be produced, such as the M&E and D&E. See also *M&E* and *D&E.*

Stock footage: Footage available from a *stock house* that may be purchased for use instead of shooting from scratch; often used for establishing shots of famous locations.

Stock house: A supplier of stock footage.

Storyboard: A series of drawings showing the composition of each shot in a sequence or film or an animation.

Streaming video: A system of recording only the changing elements of a video frame, thereby greatly reducing the amount of data needed.

Submaster: An exact copy of a videotape; made to protect the master in case of damage.

Supervising sound editor: The person who guides the film through the audio portion of postproduction.

Sweetening: Simplified audio work that is done to a program to smooth the audio.

Sync point: The point marked simultaneously on the film and the sound recording, through the use of a clapstick, to establish the point at which sound and picture are perfectly synchronized.

Take: A version of a shot.

Telecine: The machine or process that transfers film images to videotape.

Temp dub: A sound effects and music track that is supplied for preview screenings and is more complete than the temp music that may have been added earlier.

Temporary music and effects: Music and effects that are inserted by the editor in an early version of the film to enhance it and perhaps to give an impression of what may be intended for the final product.

3:2 pulldown: The method of transferring film to video to compensate for their differing frame rates. Four film frames become five video frames by repeating a field of visual information every other frame. Thus, three fields of information are recorded, then two, then three.

Time code: A digitally encoded signal in hours:minutes:seconds:frames (HH:MM:SS:FF).

Timer: The technician who makes adjustments in the film-printing process to achieve the desired look in each shot. The same function is served by a video timer in transferring to video.

Timing: Adjusting the color, brightness, and other aspects of the picture through adjustments in the printing process. The same decisions must be made when transferring the film to video. These processes are done by *timers*.

Tone: An audio reference signal that is used to calibrate playback.

Transfer: Translating from film to video or vice versa or from one format to another.

Trial print: A film print to test preliminary exposure settings.

24pHDTV: High-resolution wide-screen video that scans progressively at 24 frames per second. See *progressive video.*

Two-pop: An audible beep that is placed on a film or video countdown two seconds before the start of a picture.

Underscore: The music for the film.

Video time code: The reference numbers that are generated in dailies when they are transferred to videotape.

VU meter: A meter that measures the volume units of audio.

Walla: Adding the human sounds, such as crowd noises and telephone voices, that complete the world of the scene. This is the business of "loop groups."

WGA: The Writers Guild of America.

Whiteout: Fading to white.

Wide shot: A shot that includes a wide area of a scene.

Wild lines: Lines of dialogue that are recorded without picture for possible use by the editor.

Windows: The small displays of time or key codes on dailies.

Wipe: A transition from one picture to another through the use of some sort of design.

Wireframe: A preliminary form of a CGI effect in which the figures are outlined by lines connecting dots.

Workprint: The edited film of a program.

Wrap: To finish the film, or a portion of the work on a film.

Zoom: Gradual changing of the composition of a shot by moving in or out. In production, accomplished with a lens with adjustable focal lengths. In post, accomplished with an optical.

Index of Films Cited

(This list does not include television programs mentioned in the text.)

GENERAL INDEX

This index does not duplicate the topics listed in the Contents.

161